The
AQUARIUM
FISH
H A N D B O O K

The
AQUARIUM
FISH
H A N D B O O K

Mary Bailey
Nick Dakin

First published in 1998 by
New Holland Publishers (UK) Ltd
London • Cape Town • Sydney • Auckland

24 Nutford Place
London W1H 6DQ
United Kingdom

80 McKenzie Street
Cape Town 8001
South Africa

14 Aquatic Drive
Frenchs Forest, NSW 2086
Australia

218 Lake Road
Northcote, Auckland
New Zealand

ISBN 1 85368 788 X (hard cover)
ISBN 1 85974 190 8 (soft cover)

Senior Designer: Lyndall du Toit
Editor: Simon Pooley
Publishing Manager: Mariëlle Renssen
Illustrator: Steven Felmore
Consultants: Ed Bauman (USA), Prof. Mike Bruton
(South Africa) and David Crass (Australia).
Reproduction by Hirt and Carter Cape (Pty) Ltd
Printed and bound in Singapore by Tien Wah Press
(Pte) Ltd
10 9 8 7 6 5 4 3 2 1

Author's acknowledgements
The authors would like to thank: Gina Sandford for
critically reading the manuscript; Dr Keith Banister
for ichthyological information; Roman Sznober for
other scientific and technical advice; Ed Bauman
for information on US filtration systems.

Mary Bailey is grateful to Tamara Tat for her
assistance with the typing; *zikomo* to Ad Konings
and Esther and Stuart Grant for enabling her to
visit some tropical biotopes; also Jonathan Fulcher,

Sheila, Nick, Heather and Stan, who looked after the fish, house, cats, and Minnie, back in England.

Nick Dakin gives special thanks to his mother; Suzanne for her love and support; Ron and Iris for being such good friends; Terry Evans, Keith, Nick F and everyone who knows me and has helped.

Publisher's acknowledgements
Thanks to Northern Aquatics, Sam's Aquarium, and Tropicarium, for props. Thanks to Two Oceans Aquarium for equipment, décor, fish and room to photograph in. Thanks to all the Two Oceans Aquarium staff for their helpfulness, in particular Helen Lockheart. Special thanks to Billy Stanley and Paul Lötter for designing and building the biotope tanks.

Thanks to Anthony Johnson for his professionalism and for the use of his studio during the shoot, and Rodney Howard Luyt for allowing us to photograph his coral reef aquarium tank.

Thanks to Tony Stones (UK) for copy editing.

CONTENTS

INTRODUCTION

Imagine a mighty river. It starts its life as a tiny rivulet, high in the rain-drenched granite mountains of some tropical region, one of many such tiny streams tumbling down precipitous slopes to unite in the embryo river, already rushing inexorably downwards, heading for the distant ocean.

By the time it reaches the jungle below it has become a significant watercourse, swelled by further tributary streams and already worthy of the name, river. Now it winds more slowly across flatter, forest-clad terrain, its volume continually increased by other streams and rivers, its waters stained black by organic material from the trees that cloak its banks.

Another range of hills now blocks its progress. Over the eons it has cut a gorge through these limestone highlands; but its waters are nevertheless constricted into a narrower bed than before, and descend over waterfalls and rapids in a raging torrent reminiscent of those original precipitous rivulets, but on a far, far grander scale.

Next is more lowland forest, then a swampy region bordering its first estuary as our river enters a great lake – really more of an inland sea. Here its waters mingle with those brought by countless other streams, before it enters the final stage of its long journey. One more precipitous descent to the coastal lowlands, then our river makes its slow passage through brackish mangrove swamps and lagoons, already mixing with the salty waters of its destination, the sea.

Yet even now its story isn't over, for, as part of the world's oceans, its waters may break in waves on coral reefs, rocky cliffs and sandy beaches. Eventually, this water will evaporate to form clouds, to rain on some other mountain somewhere, starting the entire cycle over again.

'But what,' you may well ask, 'does this have to do with an aquarium?' The answer is simple, 'Everything!' Water is not a simple, static element – in nature it varies, often dramatically, with the circumstances in which it finds itself; and so do the fishes and other creatures which live in it.

Fishkeeping is an ancient pastime: the Chinese are thought to have been the first to keep ornamental fishes, thousands of years ago. Nevertheless the hobby only became universally popular after the growth in popularity of public aquaria in the mid-nineteenth century. For a large part of its history it has been a somewhat hit-and-miss affair, with a relatively limited number of species being kept:

Old-fashioned piston air pump.

those that were able to survive being introduced into whatever conditions their new owner provided – usually with little forethought, or even awareness that forethought might be necessary!

In recent times aquarists, and their fish, have benefited from huge steps forward in aquarium technology, which have enabled them to simulate, with relative ease, albeit often significant expense, almost any water conditions they choose. Not just fresh water – the domestic marine aquarium has become a reality, not simply a dream. And with this technological leap forward has come the increasing realization that different fish have evolved to inhabit different environments, and that even if they manage to stay alive in the unspecialized general aquarium, perhaps they might feel better, look better, and even breed, if provided with conditions reminiscent of their original home.

Water is not the only factor involved – although it remains the primary consideration. Other elements of the natural habitat such as food, cover and light all play a role. Using this approach, aquarists are now succeeding in maintaining, and often breeding, fish that were considered impossible to keep only a couple of decades ago. This has not only greatly increased the variety of species available to aquarists, but has encouraged the collection of more and

more new species. The basic aquarium filled with local tap water and 'hardy' freshwater tropical fish is still extremely popular, but the availability – and hence public visibility – of more exotic species is leading more and more aquarists to thoughts of something more specialized.

So let us look again at our river in this new light. Consider how different conditions must be in each major stage of its journey; whether it be its long meanderings through rainforests, its tumultuous descent through mountain gorges, its passage through the huge freshwater lake or the brackish coastal mangrove swamps. Each of these habitats has its own different water conditions, geology, flora and fauna (not just the fish) – the whole adding up to what is termed a 'biotope', a habitat and the living things it contains.

Above *Great leaps forward in aquarium technology, together with advances in our understanding of the needs of fish, have made the domestic marine aquarium a possibility.*

The oceans likewise contain many different biotopes, although of all their rich and varied inhabitants it is chiefly the brightly coloured coral reef dwellers that have captured the attention of the amateur aquarist.

We will return to our river from time to time throughout this book, as any aquarium, whether a basic general community of hardy species, or a specialized biotope simulation, is governed by the laws and processes of Nature, even though its owner may not realize this fact. How much better the chances of success, given an understanding of the natural processes taking place!

Left *Table-top aquaria were popular in the latter half of the nineteenth century.*

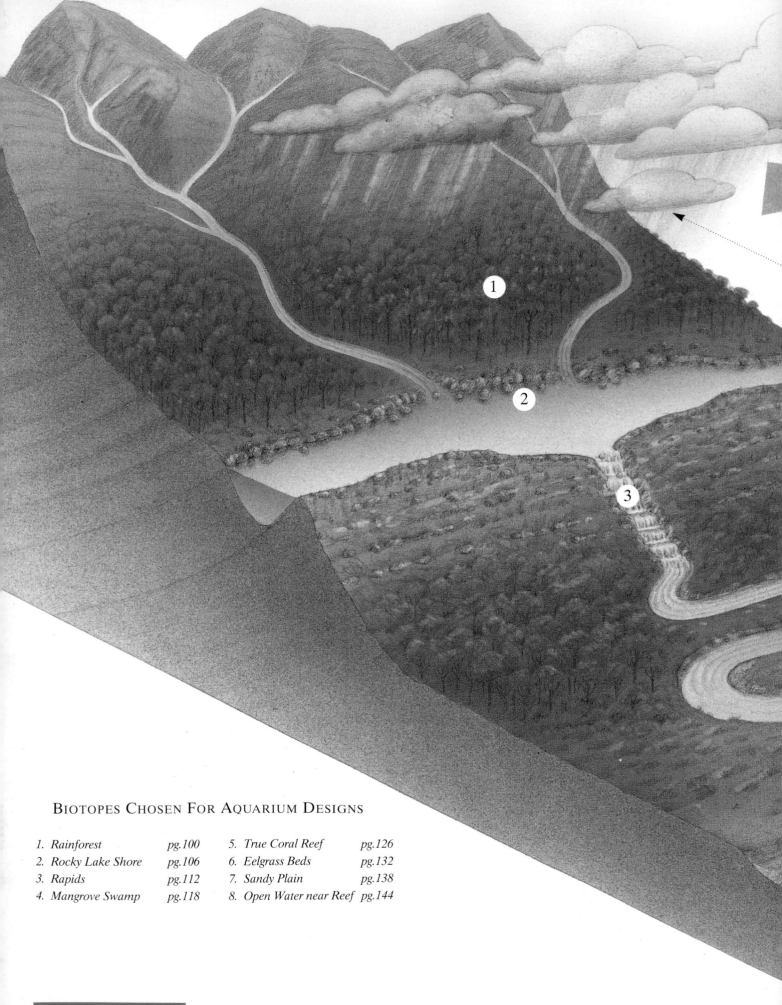

BIOTOPES CHOSEN FOR AQUARIUM DESIGNS

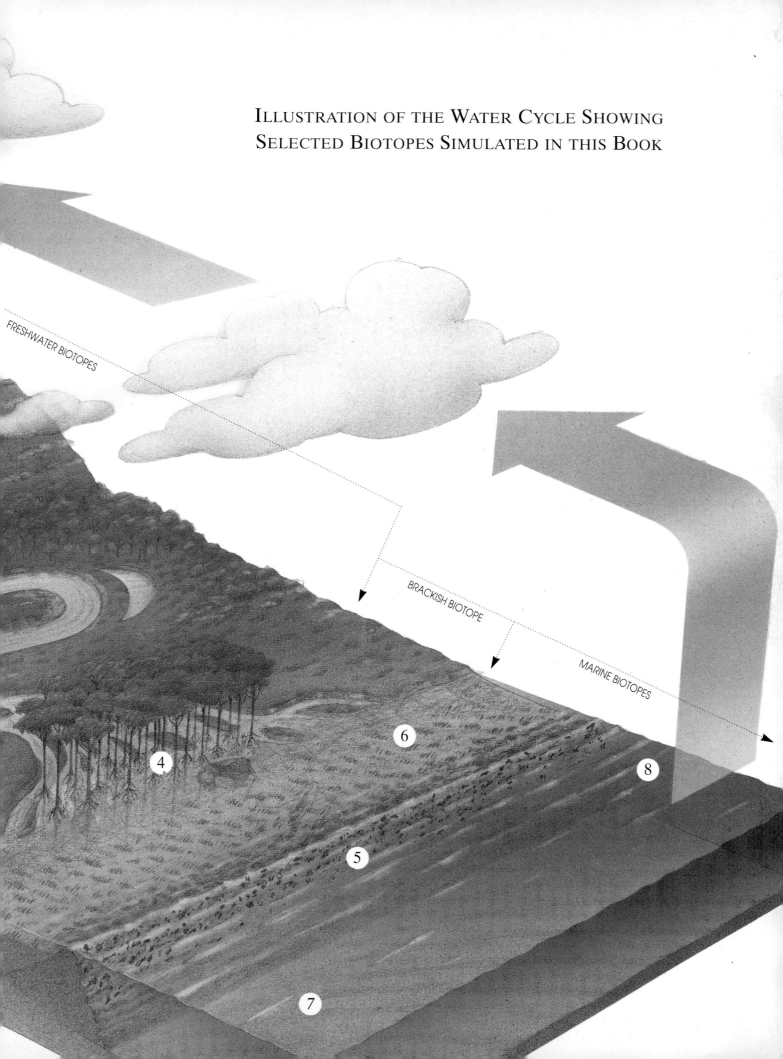

ILLUSTRATION OF THE WATER CYCLE SHOWING
SELECTED BIOTOPES SIMULATED IN THIS BOOK

FRESHWATER BIOTOPES

BRACKISH BIOTOPE

MARINE BIOTOPES

CHAPTER ONE

WATER CHEMISTRY, QUALITY AND FILTRATION

All life forms rely on water for their survival – none more so than those which live in it – and cannot survive for even a short time without it. Fishes and other aquatic organisms are almost entirely reliant on this element for their existence, and a basic understanding of its qualities is therefore necessary for the successful long-term maintenance of any aquarium.

Pure water consists of hydrogen and oxygen and nothing else, but natural water invariably contains natural 'contaminants', derived from the air through which rain falls, the ground over which rivers flow, and organic material from plants and animals living – and dying – in and around it. Nowadays water is, of course, also increasingly contaminated by the organic and inorganic pollutants created by humankind.

Aquatic organisms from a particular body of water will commonly have evolved metabolisms designed to deal with, and in fact utilize, the natural contaminants found there. Without these they may fail to thrive or even die, just as they may fall sick and perish in the presence of other, unfamiliar pollutants. Sudden changes can result in rapid death from toxic shock.

From this it should be evident that it is desirable, and in some cases essential, to keep fish in the type of water that they naturally inhabit, although there are a number of 'hardy' species that

Wreckfish swimming close to a reef wall. To recreate this scene will require a grasp of water chemistry and quality.

will tolerate, or adapt to, a variety of conditions.

The 'alien' substances dissolved in any sample of water constitute its **chemistry**. In aquarium terminology, water chemistry usually relates to naturally occurring or deliberately introduced (by the aquarist) inorganic or organic substances, and in particular to the quantity of such substances in the water, and their acidifying or alkalising effect.

Water **quality**, on the other hand, is a measure of the presence or absence of undesirable and potentially harmful materials (chiefly organic). Test kits and equipment are available for measuring various aspects of both the chemistry and quality of aquarium water.

Testing the hardness of the aquarium water.

WATER CHEMISTRY

Water chemistry is generally divided into three main sections: hardness, pH, and, for brackish/salt water, salinity.

HARDNESS

Water which contains few or no dissolved minerals is termed mineral-depleted or mineral-poor, while water which has a high content of dissolved mineral salts (e.g. carbonates, bicarbonates, chlorides and sulphates), usually acquired by flowing over soluble or partially soluble rocks such as limestones, is termed mineral-rich.

Hardness was originally the measure of the ability of water to produce a lather with soap, and is usually expressed in terms of calcium carbonate ($CaCO_3$) content, measured in degrees (dH) or parts per million (ppm). It is possible for water to test as soft (i.e. containing little $CaCO_3$) yet be rich in other minerals, a distinction rarely acknowledged by aquarists, but one which it is vital to appreciate. Many species generally described as 'soft water' fish in fact come from waters which are not only soft but also mineral-

MEASUREMENT OF HARDNESS

The definition of degrees of hardness is, unfortunately, not universal and often varies from country to country and from test kit to test kit. The following table compares the widely used German scale with an alternative method based on milligrams of $CaCO_3$ per litre of water (parts per million, or ppm):

dH	mg/litre CaCO₃ (approx.)	Description
0–3	0–50	soft
3–6	50–100	slightly hard
6–12	100–200	moderately hard
12–18	200–300	very hard
18 +	300 +	extremely hard

CONVERSION FACTORS:

1 English degree of hardness (dH) = 14.3 ppm $CaCO_3$

1 American degree of hardness = 17.1 ppm $CaCO_3$

1 German degree of hardness = 17.9 ppm $CaCO_3$

1 French degree of hardness = 10.0 ppm $CaCO_3$

It is clearly important to know what scale your test kit uses in order to obtain an accurate idea of relative hardness. Hardness figures quoted in this book are in German dH.

poor. This is an important point, because some methods of softening water simply change calcium carbonate to different salts, and do not decrease overall mineral content at all.

While fish originating in hard water can sometimes adapt to softer conditions, soft water species often fare very badly in hard water.

pH

The pH scale is a universally recognized measurement of acidity and alkalinity, whether applied to soil, chemicals or water. Fish become adapted to a particular pH in the wild and generally fare better when this is replicated in the aquarium. Indeed, many fish will refuse to breed unless the correct pH is duplicated. Nevertheless tank-bred fish are often raised in a pH that would otherwise be alien to them, having eventually, after a number of generations, adapted to tolerate a wide range of pH.

pH is measured on a scale of 0–14: 0 represents extremely potent acids; 14 is a measurement of absolute alkalinity; and 7 is neutral. Each increment of 1 unit is subdivided into 10 smaller divisions (e.g. 2, 2.1 2.2–2.9, 3). The scale is also logarithmic, i.e. pH 8 is 10 times more alkaline than pH 7, and 100 times more alkaline than pH 6. In the case of a fish used to pH 5.5, a sudden transfer to pH 7.5 will pose a shock liable to severely distress the fish or, more likely, to kill it outright.

The pH of water may be affected by its mineral content (hard and alkaline conditions generally go hand in hand), or by the quantity of acidifying carbon dioxide and the organic material it contains; or both combining to produce fairly neutral conditions.

The vast majority of fish species are found in waters within the pH range 4–9, each having adapted over many thousands of years to a particular value, or at least to a relatively small range. Very few freshwater fish live in biotopes where there is an annual variation of more than 0.5. Consequently, it goes without saying that the aquarist must do his/her best to match the pH in the aquarium to that found in the wild.

While such provisions are not always necessary or possible in the basic general community aquarium of hardy species (see Chapter Two), in most cases it is best to avoid housing species which originate from acidic, neutral and alkaline waters together in the same tank.

Whereas the pH of fresh water is geographically highly variable, marine fish live in an environment where the pH remains steady at approximately 8.3 the world over (as the seas and oceans are a single connected body of water). Needless to say, any marked variance here, i.e. outside the range pH 7.9–8.5, could be highly detrimental to the health of the fish.

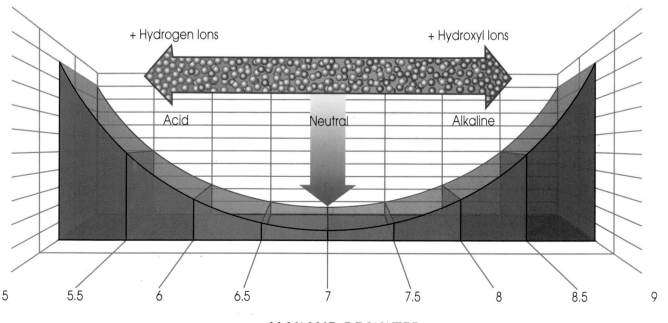

+ Hydrogen Ions   + Hydroxyl Ions

Acid   Neutral   Alkaline

5   5.5   6   6.5   7   7.5   8   8.5   9

pH VALUE OF WATER

Specific gravity
reading point

Temperature
safety zone

HYDROMETER

Above *A hydrometer is used to measure the salinity of a marine aquarium.*

Right *The headwaters of a river in the mountains, where pure, cool streams gather to form the embryo river.*

SALINITY

The salinity of water is the measure of its saltiness – to all intents and purposes, the amount of sodium chloride (NaCl, or common salt) present, as this is by far the largest component.

Salinity is commonly measured in parts per thousand (ppt), and as most tropical seas have a salinity of 35 ppt this is easily expressed as 35g of salt to 1kg (= 1 litre) of water (or 6oz per gal.). (1 gal. = 1.2 US gal.) However, most marine aquarists prefer to use a hydrometer and measure the density of the water, expressed in terms of its specific gravity (S.G.): the ratio between the density (the ratio of weight to volume) of salt water (or any substance) – and that of distilled water (which is given the value 1.0). The

addition of salt increases the S.G., and the denser the water (with dissolved salt), the higher a hydrometer will float in the solution, as it becomes increasingly buoyant. Once properly calibrated, the scale on the hydrometer can be read against the surface of the water and the specific gravity established. SG varies with temperature, so that 35 ppt = SG 1.026 at 15°C (59°F), and SG 1.0236 at 25°C (77°F).

Brackish Water
There are no rules as to what constitutes brackish water as, in the wild, the salinity is constantly in flux. It is simply a point between salt-free fresh water and full-strength sea water, and may vary from 5–30 ppt (SG approximately 1.001–1.021 at 20°C; 68°F).

Many brackish water aquarists maintain their salinity at about half that of the marine aquarium (SG 1.020), i.e. SG 1.010. This approximates to 15g NaCl per litre (2.5oz per gal.).

A TRIP DOWN THE RIVER

To demonstrate how water chemistry works in nature, let us take a break from the technicalities, and make a trip down our imaginary river to see what happens there.

Like many great rivers, ours has its beginnings high in the mountains, where rain and sometimes melting snow rapidly accumulates to feed fast-flowing streams. As they converge into a common course, these clear streams soon form a recognizable

embryo river, whose water is fresh and almost completely untainted by either organic or inorganic material. Very few creatures inhabit this cold and inhospitable world.

Cool, fresh water is the very lifeblood of our river and remains an essential source of revitalization, in complete contrast to the silt-laden waters that will finally end their days flowing through the mangrove swamps and ultimately to the sea.

ORGANIC ACIDIFICATION

As our embryo river gains strength from the multitude of streams feeding it, we find that the chemistry of the water has started to alter. Copious amounts of rain have reacted with atmospheric carbon dioxide to form dilute carbonic acid. The tannins from decaying leaf litter help to acidify the water further, often turning it brown. In addition, the river has broadened and its progress is more sluggish and stately. As a result, dissolved carbon dioxide levels are increased further, much to the benefit of plants, which thrive in the presence of this gas.

At this stage, the river has not yet run over soluble rocks such as limestone and is thus devoid of the mineral salts that impart hardness. Its water is soft and acidic, typical of many rainforest biotopes. Under the protection of lush plant growth, fish and other organisms flourish, making this one of the most productive regions for fish species and other aquatic life on Earth.

Above *A river meanders through a rainforest region, its waters stained brown by tannins from decaying leaf litter.*

intermingle as its waters meet the rising tide. Silt and other particles cannot be held in suspension in the now sluggish current, and drift to the bottom to form a muddy substrate, well suited to the growth of mangroves. These trees form an ever denser barrier, slowing the waters still further and enabling even more nutrient-rich silt to drop out of suspension. The result is a luxuriant mangrove swamp – not a disease-ridden landscape, stinking and useless, as some would have us believe, but an invaluable nursery area for the young of marine fish and invertebrates. It has its own specialized flora and fauna, in addition to salt-tolerant visitors from the fresh waters upstream and migrants from the salty waters of the sea.

The mixture of fresh water from our river and salt water from the ocean produces brackish water. Neither fully marine, nor fully fresh, and varying with every tide and flood-producing storm upriver, it creates an unusual habitat for many unique species.

Above *The waters of Lake Malawi at Nkata Bay. Surrounding rocks have been dissolved by the rivers and streams which feed into the lake, and as a result the water is hard and alkaline.*

Right *Mangrove trees thrive in the slow-flowing, brackish waters – where the fresh water of a river mingles with the salty water of the sea.*

THE EFFECTS OF LIMESTONE

As our river flows into the huge lake, its chemistry is altered once again. The rocks in and around the lake are soluble limestone, and, over the eons, have dissolved, releasing part of their mineral content into the water. The myriad streams feeding the lake have also played their part in eroding the surrounding rocks and reinforcing this high mineral content.

The result is a lake with very hard alkaline water – quite the opposite of the rainforest river, and home to a totally different flora and fauna, which have adapted to the local conditions.

Leaving the lake behind it, the river becomes a little softer and less alkaline as a result of the influence of rain (which dilutes the hardness) and acidifying organic matter, as well as the influx of soft water tributaries. However, with the mineral salt burden acquired in the lake, it can never regain the specialized conditions of the rainforest above the lake.

AN INFLUX OF SALT

The next major change takes place as the landscape begins once more to flatten, as we approach the coastal lowlands and our river broadens and slows within sight of the sea. Fresh and salt water begin to

THE OCEAN

Eventually, our well-travelled waters mix with and form part of the oceans. Having parted with most of their load of silt and food particles in the mangrove swamps and tidal flats, our river's clear waters now spread over the coral reefs that surround the shallow coastal regions. Here we come to the end of our journey in one of the most colourful and species-rich habitats on Earth.

Fresh water now gives way to full-strength sea water, which covers approximately 70% of the Earth's surface and is composed of identical substances everywhere. You may be surprised to learn that 99% of the mineral content of natural sea water is composed of just seven salts. Sodium chloride (NaCl) is by far the most abundant at 85.5%; magnesium chloride ($MgCl_2$), magnesium sulphate ($MgSO_4$), calcium sulphate ($CaSO_4$), potassium sulphate (KSO_4), calcium carbonate ($CaCO_3$) and sodium bromide (NaBr) constitute the

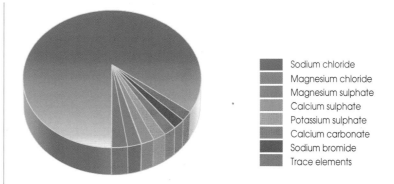

- Sodium chloride
- Magnesium chloride
- Magnesium sulphate
- Calcium sulphate
- Potassium sulphate
- Calcium carbonate
- Sodium bromide
- Trace elements

MINERAL CONTENT OF NATURAL SEA WATER

bulk of the remainder, each in much smaller quantities but always in the same proportion. The 1% balance is made up of numerous trace elements.

Although certain seas have been measured as saltier than others, this is because of an increased evaporation rate continuously reducing their water content, rather than any inherently higher salt concentration here. In the ocean, constantly fluctuating water parameters give way to stability in all things. Temperature, salinity, hardness and pH all remain relatively unchanged over long periods of time.

ADJUSTING WATER CHEMISTRY

Few aquarists have tap water which is ideally suited to the fishes they wish to keep. There are however steps that can be taken to modify this to create the correct conditions.

Hardening aquarium water is generally a straightforward matter of introducing calcareous (i.e. $CaCO_3$-rich) décor materials such as tufa rock and coral sand. Proprietary salts are now widely available to replicate the chemistry of hard water lakes such as Lakes Malawi and Tanganyika. These are *not* 'marine' salt formulations, which are unsuitable; 'salt' is here used in its chemical sense (e.g. sulphates, chlorides, carbonates etc.).

SOFTENING WATER

Aquarists in hard alkaline water areas who want to keep or breed species that prefer soft acidic water, will need to soften their water before use. This is not as simple as increasing the hardness. A number of methods, of variable efficacy and requiring variable injections of money or effort, are available.

ACTIVATED CARBON

Carbon has long been known for its purifying qualities when used in air-conditioning units. In the aquarium it can be equally useful for removing harmful substances and some medications, as well as organics that turn the water yellow. 'Activated' carbon is the most efficient, and preferable for marine applications. It is fired twice, or treated with phosphoric acid, to increase the number of microscopic pores – and hence the surface area available to adsorb unwanted substances. Its effectiveness is finite, however, and it requires regular replacement (depending on 'loading').

Water Softening Resins
Proprietary water softening (ion exchange) resins are available, hard water being passed through the resin to emerge as soft. Unfortunately, during this process calcium (Ca) ions are usually exchanged for sodium (Na) ions, so although the resulting water is soft, it is still mineral-rich and unsuitable for most 'soft water' species.

Rain Water
Alternatively, the aquarist can collect rain water, which is mineral depleted, usually has a neutral or slightly acid pH, and can be easily influenced to become more acidic. The disadvantage of this method is air pollution from the emissions of cars, industry etc., which contaminates the falling rain and renders it quite unsuitable for fish!

Unless you are certain that rain water in your area is free of, or low in, airborne contaminants, it may be better to forego its collection, although rain collected well into a lengthy heavy downpour, after the air has been 'washed' clean, is usually safe to use.

It should be collected only from roofs which will not affect its chemistry or quality, and gutters should be kept clean. Ideally it should be strained through activated carbon to remove any residual contaminants.

Rain water can be used 'neat' or to dilute the hardness of tap water.

Pure H_2O
The safest and most effective method of providing soft water is to use water which has been distilled, de-ionized, or passed through a reverse osmosis (RO) unit (see below). Each method removes *all* contaminants leaving pure H_2O, which is normally mixed with at least some tap water in order to provide a minimal mineral content, and stabilize the pH (see below). Remember that all contaminants are removed, including the free oxygen that fishes breathe, so the water must be aerated before use or they will literally suffocate.

In addition to removing mineral salts, all three methods remove organic contaminants – useful if your tap water quality is less than optimal.

Distilled Water
Distilled water can be obtained from pharmacies and laboratory supply companies, but it is expensive and rarely used for aquaria.

De-ionizers
De-ionizers normally use two ion-exchange resins; one exchanges anions (negatively-charged ions), and the other cations (positively-charged ions) in an aqueous solution, removing almost all organic and inorganic substances. While initially very efficient, both resins are quickly exhausted and require frequent recharging or replacement.

Reverse Osmosis (RO)
In recent years this new method of purifying tap water has found great favour with marine aquarists because of its ability to remove in excess of 95% of *all* substances held in solution, including pesticides, bacteria, heavy metals and dissolved organics. It utilizes a thin film composite (TFC) membrane, through which only water molecules can pass. All other molecules are excluded and the result is water as pure as could be expected from a cloudburst over the mountains.

Below *Unit and storage container for reverse osmosis.*

Hard water may also be partially softened by boiling. This removes temporary hardness (caused by bicarbonates), but permanent ($CaCO_3$) hardness remains.

It is essential to avoid using décor items which will add hardness to your hard-won soft water.

MODIFYING pH

Increasing pH is normally simply a matter of adding calcareous material to the aquarium. Bicarbonate of soda, added in solution in small doses (you need to test the tank pH between doses), can also be used, especially if a quick result is required.

Acidifying the Water

Reducing the pH of soft water (trying to reduce that of hard water is a waste of time, as it will revert as quickly as you can modify it!) is best achieved by peat filtration (see below) until the target is reached, although water changes will probably mean that some degree of peat filtration is constantly required.

Some types of aquarium peat are more 'active' than others, some reducing pH slowly whilst others make it drop dramatically. Obviously the latter must not be used in an aquarium containing fish. Only pure peat should be used; horticultural moss peat is acceptable – and cheap – but only types without additives such as fertilizers should be used.

Alternatively, pack a nylon bag (you can use pantihose) with peat and soak it in a bucket of soft water; the tannins it contains will leach into the water and the resulting extract can be added to the aquarium water as required. You can also boil up peat in water (avoid any pan, e.g. those made of aluminium, which is likely to cause metallic contamination), to provide peat extract. In both cases add a little at a time and test the tank pH after each dose.

Proprietary products of a similar nature are available but these are usually considerably more expensive.

Chemical pH Adjusters

It is also possible to purchase proprietary chemical pH adjusters. These must always be used in accordance with the manufacturer's instructions, and even then there are sometimes unexpected side-effects. Natural methods of adjusting pH are safer and thus preferable.

pH Buffering

The metabolic byproducts of fish and plants have a constant slight acidifying effect, so it is wise to monitor the pH regularly to ensure that it doesn't drop suddenly or too far. It is wise to include some calcareous décor in hard water tanks to 'buffer' the pH against this gentle acidification – as acids are produced they dissolve the $CaCO_3$ and the pH rises again.

The pH of extremely mineral-poor water can be very unstable and fluctuate widely, a state of affairs not generally enjoyed by its occupants. Again the answer is to include a small amount of calcareous material as a stabilizing buffer.

CREATING SALT OR BRACKISH WATER

Only specially formulated 'marine salt' should be used for this purpose, mixed with good quality fresh water (ideally RO) according to the manufacturer's instructions. Domestic salt may contain harmful additives and is *not* suitable.

ADDITIONAL WATER PARAMETERS

OXYGEN CONTENT

We have already seen how our river tends to be high in carbon dioxide where it is slow-moving; contrast the situation in our lake, effectively an inland sea, with waves and surf increasing gas exchange at the surface, driving off carbon dioxide and enabling the water to absorb large amounts of free oxygen from the atmosphere. The same happens in the sea.

Again, at the far end of our imaginary lake, the river passes over relatively shallow rapids, where the water boils and churns as it displays its force, smashing against the rocks and boulders just below the surface. Eventually the water is channelled through a gorge and over a waterfall in an endless bout of activity. This, too, leads to a high oxygen content.

In all these cases the constant creation of new interfaces between air and water provides an almost continuous opportunity for oxygen to enter the water and carbon dioxide to leave it. Many fish living in

Carbon dioxide cylinder.

these areas where oxygen is supersaturated find it extremely difficult to survive should the dissolved oxygen content fall below a certain level.

Aerating the aquarium usually requires no more effort than providing a reasonable amount of water circulation. Contrary to popular belief, passing a stream of air bubbles through the water does not 'force' oxygen into the water, it merely encourages water circulation, bringing the bottom oxygen-depleted layers to the top, to be re-oxygenated by gas exchange at the surface. Movement of the water's surface will increase the rate at which gas exchange can take place, and is usually achieved by means of the filtration (see below) outlet or outlets, sometimes augmented by aeration using an air pump (see Chapter Three).

CO_2 DOSING

In the course of photosynthesis, plants utilize carbon dioxide (CO_2). Aquatic plants are no different, except that the CO_2 is available as a dissolved gas in the water rather than taken from the air.

Many hobbyists with an interest in plants find that introducing CO_2 gas into the aquarium has a beneficial effect on plant growth. A pressurized CO_2 cylinder feeds a small container in the aquarium where bubbles of carbon dioxide can be observed. By controlling the amount of bubbles, the quantity of dissolved CO_2 can be regulated. Great care must be taken, however, as the CO_2 content of water adversely affects its ability to absorb atmospheric oxygen, and will also have an acidifying effect, so both pH and CO_2 levels require constant careful monitoring. It is inadvisable to use CO_2 in tanks containing fish with a high oxygen requirement.

TEMPERATURE

Temperature is crucial where fish are concerned. Most fish are unable to generate body heat like mammals and have no choice but to adopt the temperature of their immediate environment. Such creatures are known as poikilotherms, or 'cold-blooded'.

Most fish have an optimum temperature at which their bodily functions can be performed most efficiently; if the temperature falls, the fish's metabolism slows and it behaves sluggishly, while if it rises, the fish's metabolic rate increases, as manifested by increased appetite and respiratory rate. Unfortunately, the warmer the water becomes, the less free

oxygen it can contain, so that the delicate gills have to work even harder for the fish to breathe at all, and the fish may actually suffocate. In fact, this fate generally befalls fish in tanks where the thermostat fails 'on'; they suffocate long before they actually 'cook'. Always remember that abnormally high or low temperatures outside an acceptable range for any given species can result in death.

Generally speaking, large volumes of water, such as large lakes and the sea, retain heat very efficiently and remain within a relatively restricted temperature range. In tropical climates, temperature variations in such bodies of water are usually relatively small and the fish may react badly to wider variations than their bodies have evolved to accept.

Within river systems, wide temperature variations may be the norm as they are affected by wet and dry seasons. In the dry season, water becomes slow-flowing, warm and oxygen-depleted. With the return of the rains, fresh, cool, well-oxygenated water floods into the river systems, acting as a trigger for a breeding frenzy for many species. The accompanying drop in temperature (this does not apply to tropical climes, such as Australia) signals a return to an environment rich in microscopic organisms to feed the hungry fry.

Rivers, being relatively shallow, may also be heated significantly by the sun during the course of the day, cooling again at night, although shade from surrounding forest will greatly reduce this effect.

WATER QUALITY

Water quality is affected by two main factors: firstly, contaminants (organic and inorganic) which it contains when drawn from the tap, and secondly those which enter it while it is in the aquarium. Both inorganic and organic contaminants are involved.

INORGANIC CONTAMINANTS

Tap water may contain small quantities of various metallic salts, either naturally or as the result of environmental pollution. It may also become contaminated with lead or copper from domestic pipework, and for this reason water from the hot water cylinder, or water that has stood in the pipes for some time, should not be used.

Chemicals used by water companies to kill bacteria (chlorine and chloramine) and crustaceans are also toxic. Water companies are required to provide water with safe levels of contaminants, but

Thermometers

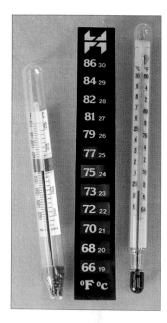

unfortunately what is 'safe' for humans may be lethal to delicate fish.

PURIFYING TAP WATER

The simplest way of making tap water safe for hardy tropical fish is to add a conditioner to remove, or nullify, the effects of chlorine and chloramines; if only chlorine is present (ask the water company) then it will dissipate if the water is allowed to stand overnight, preferably with aeration, or can often be driven off by running the tap hard into a bucket. Some conditioners also nullify other toxins, e.g. metallic salts; not all conditioners remove all toxins, so always buy one appropriate to your needs.

To improve tap water still further, we can use special resins (available from aquatic dealers), usually in special tap water treatment filters, to remove nitrates, phosphates and sulphates – all of which are less than conducive to fish health and can encourage unsightly algae in both freshwater and marine aquaria.

IN-TANK POLLUTION

In-tank inorganic contamination may derive from unsuitable décor or equipment (see Chapter Three), or the accidental influx of chemicals (such as cigarette smoke, insecticide sprays, aerosol furniture polish, paint fumes etc.). While to our knowledge no smoker has ever been implicated in the demise of any fish (at least through smoking!), most other extraneous toxins are (often quickly) lethal, and prevention is the only remedy.

ORGANIC CONTAMINATION

Organic contaminants may be present in tap water, usually derived from agricultural fertilizers or resulting from the impossibility (at least affordably) of totally purifying recycled water. Aquarists whose water comes from rivers, or river-fed reservoirs, should be particularly vigilant. Artesian supplies and rain (or spring) water reservoirs are generally more pure.

Organic pollution within the aquarium comes mainly from the metabolic processes of its occupants (plants and animals). This pollution is controlled by the nitrogen cycle, and an understanding of the latter is essential to the aquarist.

THE NITROGEN CYCLE

The nitrogen cycle is the means by which waste products are dealt with biologically by Nature, both in the wild and in our aquaria.

The first part of the cycle deals with the decomposition of the remains of plants and animals, and the excreta of the latter. These are initially broken down into highly toxic ammonia (also excreted by fish) and associated compounds, which form the diet

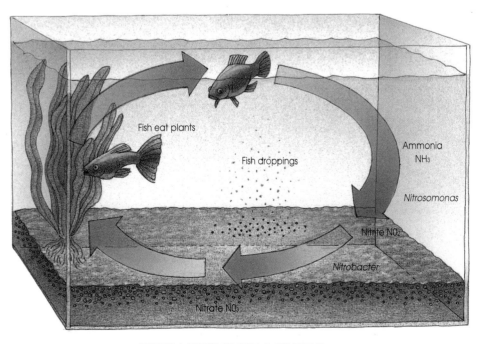

Fish eat plants

Fish droppings

Ammonia NH₃

Nitrosomonas

Nitrite NO₂

Nitrobacter

Nitrate NO₃

THE NITROGEN CYCLE

of a genus of bacteria called *Nitrosomonas*. These bacteria convert the highly toxic ammonia to slightly less toxic nitrite in the first stage of the cycle.

Next, another genus of bacteria, called *Nitrobacter*, convert nitrite into nitrate. Nitrate is not particularly harmful to most fish in reasonable quantities, though tolerance levels vary from species to species. It may be used in part by plants as natural fertilizer.

Both *Nitrosomonas* and *Nitrobacter* bacteria are aerobic, i.e. they need oxygen to survive, breed and perform their tasks. In Nature – and in the aquarium – they inhabit any suitable surface such as rocks, wood, sand, gravel and plant leaves.

Ammonia, nitrite and nitrate cannot be seen in the aquarium water, but test kits are available to test for the presence of all three.

ULTRAVIOLET (UV) STERILIZATION

In tropical latitudes the intense sunlight is an extremely potent force. Not only does it have the direct ability to scorch the Earth, but its invisible radiation can perform a sterilizing task. Harmful bacteria and viruses can be destroyed by prolonged exposure to certain portions of the spectrum.

Radiant energy arriving from the sun is composed of various elements of the spectrum. We see a very small proportion of the latter as visible light, in the region of 380–760 nanometers (nm). At either end of the visible spectrum there are additional, invisible wavelengths – ultraviolet at the blue end, and infrared at the red end.

It has long been known that ultraviolet light with a wave length of 254nm has a distinctly germicidal effect and is undoubtedly responsible for the demise of various harmful organisms which exist in shallow water. These may include the various microscopic free-swimming stages of certain fish parasites, bacteria and fungal spores, as well as unicellular algae.

Marine aquarists in particular have learnt to harness ultraviolet light to destroy many unwanted organisms in the aquarium, especially those responsible for a variety of fish diseases. There is no logical reason why the technique cannot be applied to fresh water, but this is rarely necessary and may reduce or eliminate the natural immunity of freshwater fish, which, if sold to aquarists lacking such equipment, might then succumb to each and every relatively harmless pathogen present in their new home!

Ultraviolet light is generated using a UV sterilizer, consisting of a special bulb encased in a unit that enables aquarium water to pass within 6mm (¼in) of the light source (see below). If the distance were increased, harmful organisms would not be destroyed. The flow rate past the lamp and cleanliness of the water must also be regulated carefully to produce optimum results. Ultraviolet sterilizers are best operated continuously, and the bulb should be replaced every six months.

Warning: Ultraviolet light can cause damage to the human eye and should never be looked at directly.

FILTRATION

In Nature, the processes of the nitrogen cycle are continuous and create a balance (unless major outside pollution occurs). In the aquarium, however, owing to the limited volume of water and high stocking ratios which would never be encountered in the wild, waste from our fish and uneaten food can cause serious pollution. This may kill all our pets in a matter of days unless we give Nature a helping hand by using a filtration system.

The filtration system usually operates mechanically (to collect solid wastes in one place, i.e. the filter, partly to keep the tank looking clean) and biologically (i.e. by optimizing the nitrogen cycle). In addition, chemical filtration can be used to remove some toxins, usually by adsorption (the toxin is taken up by the chemical). Chemical filtration can also be used to modify water chemistry, for example, peat filtration.

FILTER MEDIA

There are a number of different types of aquarium filter, but all use the same principle, namely passing water through a material which traps solids, sometimes 'traps' dissolved wastes chemically, and in addition provides surfaces which nitrogen cycle bacteria can colonize. Such materials are termed 'filter media' (singular 'medium'), and a huge variety of these is available.

Typical mechanical media are filter floss (spun polyester), plastic foam, gravel and sand. Media may be fine, medium or coarse in texture to suit the application. Obviously, fine media will clog up and impede flow more quickly than coarse ones. A purely mechanical filter requires cleaning extremely frequently, otherwise the trapped particles remain in contact with, and may pollute, the tank water. However, it is usual to allow a mechanical filter to develop into a biological one.

BIOLOGICAL FILTRATION

Any medium designed to provide a home for the various nitrogen cycle bacteria that 'digest' waste products is known as a biological medium. As we have already seen, the bacteria require a surface on which to live and multiply, and the larger that surface, the larger the bacterial population, given adequate quantities of oxygen and 'food'. For aquarium purposes we need a medium that has a large surface area, is preferably inert, will allow the passage of water without becoming clogged rapidly, and is readily colonized by bacteria.

Media suitable for biological filters include sand, gravel, sintered glass, various ceramic and plastic shapes, foam, coral sand and gravel, as well as various expanded clay products. All of these will also act mechanically, just as the mechanical media listed earlier will act biologically if they are left undisturbed. Obviously, some media, such as coral sand or gravel, will influence the chemistry of the water and should therefore be used only where appropriate.

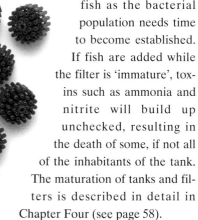

Plastic filter medium: these shapes trap solids and are colonized by nitrogen cycle bacteria.

A newly installed biological filter is incapable of supporting fish as the bacterial population needs time to become established. If fish are added while the filter is 'immature', toxins such as ammonia and nitrite will build up unchecked, resulting in the death of some, if not all of the inhabitants of the tank. The maturation of tanks and filters is described in detail in Chapter Four (see page 58).

CHEMICAL FILTRATION

Chemical media include activated carbon and zeolite, which remove some chemical pollutants (including some medications), and ammonia, respectively. Peat reduces pH, whereas calcareous media (e.g. coral sand, dolomite [limestone] chippings) make water more alkaline and increase the pH. Filter resins are available to remove nitrates, phosphates and numerous other substances.

As chemical filters tend to work best in a reasonable flow of water, they may also act mechanically and need periodic rinsing.

All chemical media have a useful 'life' and will require replacement or regeneration after the period recommended by the manufacturer.

OZONE

The fresh, clean smell often experienced after a thunderstorm is the result of ozone. Ozone gas has a purifying effect which can be adapted to help filter the marine aquarium. But what is ozone?

When an oxygen molecule (O_2) comes into contact with a high voltage field such as lightning, it may gain an extra atom and become the unstable gas called ozone (O_3). Because of this instability, the extra atom is eager to break its partnership and rush off to interact with other organic and inorganic molecules, such that contact with the gas has an oxidizing effect on a multitude of substances. In effect, substances such as dissolved solids can be 'burnt' out of existence.

Unfortunately, ozone can also be harmful, and must never be allowed to come into direct contact with invertebrates or fish. It is instead administered within the confines of a protein skimmer or ozone reactor after being generated in an 'ozonizer', a small unit housing a high voltage field generator through which air is pumped.

Ozone is of questionable value for the freshwater aquarium. It should not be allowed to escape into the room, as it can cause illness (e.g. nausea, headaches and depression).

TYPES OF AQUARIUM FILTER

There are many different types of aquarium filter, each with various pros and cons as regards efficiency, cost, and other factors. It is vital to realize that big and powerful isn't always best. For example, a rapid and violent turnover rate is neither necessary nor desirable in small tanks or large ones sparsely populated by calm-water fish. Large, messy fish may require fast turnover to clear up their detritus, and a large volume of media and bacteria to process it, while a large volume, low turnover filter is often adequate for even high population densities of small fish.

External Canister Filters

These consist of a plastic canister containing media, and an electric water pump, usually sited below the aquarium to allow the intake of water by siphonage through the inlet tube. The water then passes through the media and is returned to the tank via the pump. These filters are very useful as they permit biological, mechanical and chemical media to be used in any combination. Some have internal baskets to separate different media; others are 'open plan', such that different media must be separated by filter floss layers or placed in nylon net bags.

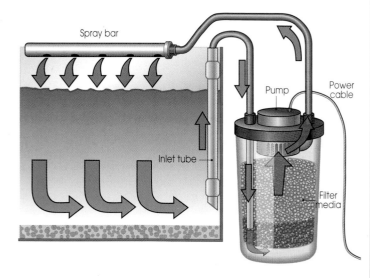

EXTERNAL
CANISTER
FILTER

In addition, canister filters can be utilized to power undergravel filters in reverse-flow or to feed above-tank trickle filters (see below).

Internal Canister Filters

These consist of a canister for media (usually plastic foam) topped by a submersible pump, the whole being immersed in the aquarium. Water is drawn in

INTERNAL CANISTER FILTER

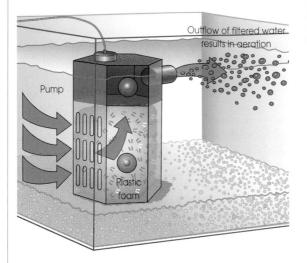

through slits in the side, or sides, of the canister and returned via the pump outlet near the top. They are available in a number of sizes and are best suited to smaller aquaria, though two or more can be used to good effect in larger tanks.

Hang-on Power Filters

This type of filter is particularly popular in the USA, where it is used by beginners in preference to canister filters. The unit consists of a plastic box filled with media that is hung on the back or side of the tank.

Water enters the filter via an intake tube that passes over the edge of the aquarium, and returns via a 'spillway', a lip moulded into the filter box that also supports the filter on the tank rim. Mechanical filtration is performed by filter floss or foam that may be part of a cartridge or formed into a pad. If this clogs, the water is pumped back into the aquarium unfiltered via a built-in bypass, to prevent overflowing. Rinsing the mechanical filter media weekly should prevent clogging. Activated carbon is used for chemical filtration – in some cases contained in a cartridge that doubles as the mechanical filter, otherwise in a pouch.

Some power filters have separate biological media that rarely, if ever, need maintenance. Other types use the mechanical and chemical media biologically, in which case these media should not both be cleaned/changed at the same time – to avoid wiping out the entire population of nitrifying bacteria.

Undergravel filter plate

Uplift tube

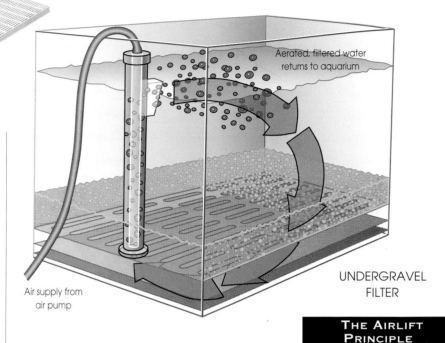

Aerated, filtered water
returns to aquarium

Air supply from
air pump

UNDERGRAVEL
FILTER

Undergravel Filters

The undergravel (UG) filter is a popular and highly effective method of biological filtration, with the advantage of a huge volume of medium and a variable flow rate.

It utilizes the vast area of the aquarium substrate (the 'filter bed') as a medium where bacteria can live and process wastes. Perforated plastic filter plates, fitted with water uplift tubes extending to near the water's surface, are positioned on the tank bottom and covered with 5 to 7.5cm (2 to 3in) of gravel and/or coarse sand (a shallower substrate depth may allow wastes to pass through, and a greater may impede flow).

Oxygenated water is continuously moved up the uplifts by the airlift effect or a powerhead (a special submersible pump), and water from the tank is pulled down through the gravel to replace it, bringing both solid and liquid wastes into contact with the bacteria in the filter bed.

One disadvantage with the so-called 'conventional' or 'downflow' system is that detritus is trapped in the substrate and can easily impede the flow of water. To overcome this, the whole system can be run in 'reverse flow', using an external canister filter packed with a medium such as filter floss. Instead of water being drawn up through the uplifts, the canister filter forces it down the tube and up through the substrate. As the filter floss traps most of the detritus particles, the substrate bed remains cleaner.

The disadvantages of this method, however, are that the 'inlet' of the filter is now the (small) inlet of the canister filter rather than the entire tank bottom, and that the bacterial population of the filter bed will be minimal as their food is in the canister! Filter efficiency is thus little, if any, better than if the canister filter were run solo as a biological filter.

Reverse-flow systems by their very nature do not encourage much water turbulence, so if a high oxygen content is required, this must be provided by separate means.

Trickle Filters

By increasing the availability of oxygen, the bacteria can be encouraged to multiply and perform their task much more efficiently. Marine aquarists in particular favour trickling water through a suitable medium without submerging it, thereby enabling the bacteria to take full advantage of oxygen in the atmosphere. It has been estimated that trickle filters can be up to 20 times more efficient than their undergravel counterparts.

Depending on the design, trickle filters can be sited above, to the side, or below the aquarium. They can also be conveniently housed in a sump that is shared with protein skimmers, pumps and other pieces of equipment to make the filtration system compact and easily accessible for maintenance.

THE AIRLIFT PRINCIPLE

When a bubble of air rises through water, it creates a slight up-current, 'lifting' water with it. A stream of bubbles, especially when confined in, for example, a tube, will create a quite significant degree of lift. This principle has long been used by aquarists to power filters of various types.

Spray bar

Aquarium water

TRICKLE FILTER

Aerated, filtered water
returns to aquarium

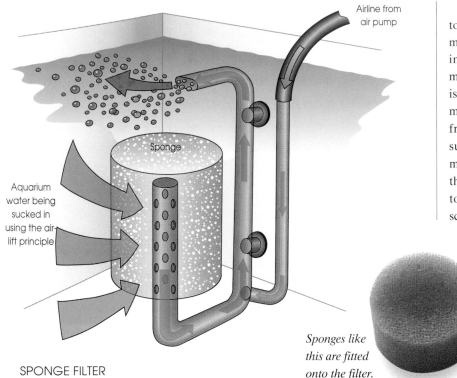

Airline from
air pump

Sponge

Aquarium
water being
sucked in
using the air-
lift principle

SPONGE FILTER

Sponges like
*this are fitted
onto the filter.*

The task of the protein skimmer is
to create an environment where the
maximum surface area is created
in the minimum space. With
most designs, a tall acrylic tube
is filled with tank water and
millions of tiny bubbles produced
from a limewood diffuser. The
surfactants are attracted to the
massive surface area supplied by
the bubbles and transported to the
top of the tube. Here, a foaming
scum is formed and rises up until it
collapses into a collection
cup. The resultant brown
liquid can then be dis-
carded.

There are various
designs of protein skimmer
but all work on the same
principle. A protein skimmer is an essential part of
any marine filtration system.

*Protein
skimmer*

Sponge Filters

Nontoxic plastic foam (sponge) makes an
excellent home for filter bacteria and a simple filter
for a small aquarium. A perforated plastic tube is
sited in the centre of a cylindrical sponge, and water
is drawn through it by means of the airlift principle.

Internal Box Filters

Internal box filters are not as popular as formerly,
having been largely superseded by canister and
sponge filters. However, they are still
available and are particularly useful
for supplementary chemical filtration, for instance filled with peat or
calciferous material to adjust pH, or
with carbon to remove some types
of medication after treatment
of disease. Internal box filters
are usually powered by the
airlift principle.

Internal box filter with peat.

PROTEIN SKIMMERS

Many organic and inorganic substances
are readily dissolved in salt water, but are
easily drawn to the interface between air
and water. Such substances are referred
to as surfactants.

Note: Most protein skimmers do not work in fresh
water as the surface tension of the water is weaker
and will not enable the quantity and quality of bubbles required to be generated.

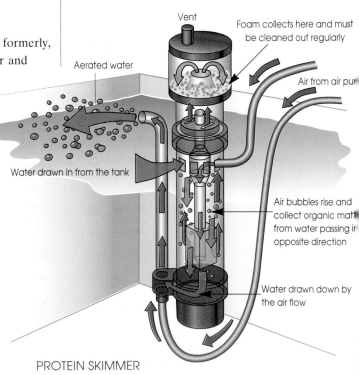

Vent

Aerated water

Water drawn in from the tank

Foam collects here and must
be cleaned out regularly

Air from air pur

Air bubbles rise and
collect organic matt
from water passing ir
opposite direction

Water drawn down by
the air flow

PROTEIN SKIMMER

WATER CHANGES

Biological filtration will make safe the ammonia and nitrite produced in the aquarium, but we are nevertheless left with an ever-increasing concentration of the end-product, nitrate.

In Nature, nitrate is eventually used up by plants, or broken down into harmless elements by an additional bacterial process difficult to replicate in the aquarium. In the short term the natural dilution factor offered by many bodies of water is important. Around most coral reefs, nitrate is barely measurable owing to the dilution effect of the vast volume of the sea. Much the same occurs in large lakes, while rivers and streams have a constant throughput of fresh water from upstream, from tributaries and springs, and from rainfall. Thus the important balance is maintained until the bacterial processes can catch up. Only in small, isolated bodies of water is serious pollution a natural hazard, and organisms from such biotopes will have evolved suitable tolerance or survival mechanisms.

Aquarium plants may remove some nitrate, but only in a densely planted aquarium with very few fishes is a balance likely to be achieved. So further intervention by the aquarist is required.

Yet again taking a leaf out of Nature's book, we can reduce nitrate (and, in emergencies, other toxins) in our aquaria by performing regular partial water changes using clean, pollutant-free water. Water changes normally involve replacing 10 to 30% of the tank volume (up to 50% in dire emergencies) with new water of the same chemistry and temperature as that of the tank, although provided the necessary adjustment is small this can be allowed to take place in the aquarium. Major sudden changes in water chemistry or temperature should, however, be avoided, as they can cause fatal shock in the fishes.

You probably didn't realize, when you decided to become a fishkeeper, that you would need to become a scientist as well. The technicalities of water management may seem frightening at this stage, but you will find that as you put them into practice you will achieve a greater understanding of the why's and wherefore's. On the other hand, ignore them at your – and your fishes' – peril!

Below *Rivers and streams have a constant throughput of fresh water from upstream, from tributaries and springs, and from rainfall. Thus the important chemical balance is maintained until the bacterial processes can catch up and deal with any build-up in natural pollutants.*

CHAPTER TWO

CHOOSING YOUR FISH

A remarkable number of people who decide that they want to keep aquarium fish, first purchase and set up an aquarium, and only then start to think about what to keep in it. Admittedly they generally decide on the type of water – fresh or salt – in advance, but that is as far as it goes at the planning stage.

Then, when they finally start to consider the aquarium's occupants, they fall in love with something quite unsuitable for the tank they have provided, and are faced with a number of unpalatable options such as starting again from scratch or keeping 'second best' fish. Worse still, some go ahead and subject a fish they would like to an environment that does not suit it at all, selfishly putting their own wishes before the welfare of the fish. How much better to make a choice of fish – and *then* provide an aquarium that is suited to them!

Many would-be aquarists go one retrograde step further. It does not occur to them that the selection of fishes they choose might not be appropriate for their aquarium; or, indeed, suitable company for each other. If they – and the fish – are lucky, the dealer will point out the error of their ways and disaster will be averted. However, not all

Damselfish (Pomacentridae).

dealers concern themselves with their customers' choice of fish.

It matters not, as far as the end result is concerned, if mistakes are made through ignorance or through deliberate negligence. Fish which are unsuitable for their environment generally end up as unhealthy, ultimately dead, fish – or

Visiting an aquarium shop can be a very enjoyable and time-consuming experience.

as large, well-rounded specimens which have devoured all of their tankmates.

Few people enjoy finding corpses littering their aquarium, or watching some favourite fish disappearing down the gullet of a new arrival, bought on impulse. How much better to find out about any proposed aquarium occupant before buying it!

THE GENERAL COMMUNITY AQUARIUM

A general community aquarium is a basic 'set-up', usually filled with local tap water and 'hardy' fishes capable of surviving a variety of conditions. It is the ideal aquarium for the beginner who has no immediate specialized fish preferences, and doesn't want a lot of 'fiddle' with water chemistry.

Top *Convict surgeon*
(Acanthurus triostegus).

Above *Killifish such as this*
Aphyosemion gardneri *are
often brightly coloured.*

Right *Freshwater fish,
such as this female*
Melanochromis chipokae,
*can be almost as striking
as marines.*

fish in the shop, is itself a community fish. It could well be a juvenile of a species that grows to 30cm (12in) or more and eats everything in its path. It might be harmless to small fish when you buy it, but give it a couple of months' growth...

At the same time, there are numerous 'exotic' species which are perfectly suited to community life, provided water conditions and décor suit them. So again, never make assumptions about fish compatibility or the lack of it; always check.

AREAS OF (IN)COMPATIBILITY

It is time to pay another visit to our river. We have already seen how water conditions may vary from biotope to biotope, and how the inhabitants of each can be expected to have metabolic processes adapted, through eons of evolution, to local water chemistry. Obviously those that have differing special requirements in this area should not be mixed; the effects of putting an acid-water fish into alkaline conditions, or vice versa, can be just as dire as putting a marine fish into fresh water. Trying to compromise – by housing acid and alkaline water fish in neutral conditions – may simply result in ill-health and suffering for both.

Less obvious, perhaps, is the fact that fish may have evolved major anatomical adaptations to water movement. For example, the fish of turbulent rapids or surf zones will generally be more streamlined than their cousins from slow-moving reaches or deeper, less agitated water. In practice, fishes from turbulent regions are often quite happy in calm water (provided it is well oxygenated), but sail-finned species, designed to glide gracefully through still or slow-moving water, may not enjoy a strong current. (See Appendix for general fish anatomy.)

Such aquaria also provide the opportunity to learn basic fishkeeping techniques before, perhaps, progressing to something more specialized. That is not to say that a beginner should not set up a specialized aquarium, provided he/she is prepared to acquire the necessary knowledge and put in the additional effort sometimes required.

This is fine in theory, but unfortunately not all the 'hardy community' species are actually compatible. Other requirements, size differences and behaviour mean some species simply aren't suited to each other's company (e.g. known fin-nippers and long-finned species!). So never make assumptions on the basis of that 'community fish' tag; always find out.

Beware too of assuming that a species you have never heard of, and which is housed with community

NATURE'S FURNITURE

A fish's surroundings may be very important to it. In a **rainforest** environment, the smaller fish (those we normally keep) are usually found along the river margins, where vegetation provides shelter; there will also be holes in the banks to hide in, and tangles of roots, dead branches, even fallen tree-trunks. The bottom is often covered with a layer of (dark) dead leaves in these bank zones.

Matters are quite different in the **rapids**. Here rocks are the main feature, with perhaps the odd piece of driftwood jammed between boulders. Higher plants cannot grow in the current. The fish of this habitat are 'cave-dwellers', living in crevices and burrowing under boulders.

The **lake**, because of its vastness, offers a number of distinct habitats: rocky shores with breaking surf, sandy shallows with beds of aquatic vegetation, open water, muddy river estuaries, and intermediate zones where major habitats meet. Such a lake will contain some generalized species which are at home anywhere, and many specialized ones in the various local biotopes.

The **mangrove swamp** is like the rainforest in many respects, but, obviously, the water chemistry is totally different. The **coral reef**, of course, is another world entirely, with a vast multicoloured array of corals, seaweeds and invertebrates, and gleaming coral sand.

Never underestimate the importance of the correct cover to any fish, especially the small ones. These creatures are near the bottom of the food chain, and their continued existence, in the wild, depends on staying near shelter and disappearing into it in emergencies. Many will be badly stressed by the absence of the correct type of cover, even if an alternative (from the aquarist's point of view) is available, and even if there are no predators in the tank. They may not recognize it as cover, or they may be the wrong shape to utilize it. A deep, laterally compressed fish designed to lurk among plant stems cannot fit into a low-ceilinged cave!

Most 'hardy community species' are psychologically as well as physically robust, and generally content with a planted aquarium, perhaps with one or two 'caves' or other items under which to shelter. Many others, however, are unlikely to thrive without the security of 'natural' surroundings. For these a biotope aquarium, with, of course, the correct water conditions as well as appropriate décor, is essential.

THE HUNTER AND THE HUNTED

A common error is to assume that because fish share a biotope in nature, they will do so in captivity. Nothing could be further from the truth!

In any biotope there is a food chain, with primitive plants and micro-organisms at the bottom of the chain, and birds and mammals at the top. In between, in the aquatic biotope, are the fish, small and large, with the latter commonly feeding on the former. They do not abandon this behaviour simply because we house them in an aquarium and offer them other things to eat! Equally, fish from different biotopes are just as likely to eat each other if the size difference makes this feasible. Some predators can eat prey up to three-quarters of their own size. So, be aware that most fish will consume anything mobile that they can fit into their mouths. Thus a group of fish need to be of roughly similar size to avoid 'accidental' predation. Even if a large fish is known to be perfectly safe with small ones, remember the latter won't know that. Do you really want them to live in perpetual terror of being eaten?

Above *Tubular sponge, home to small fish and invertebrates.*

Below *An anemonefish* (Amphiprion ocellaris) *in its anemone home.*

SCIENTIFIC AND COMMON NAMES

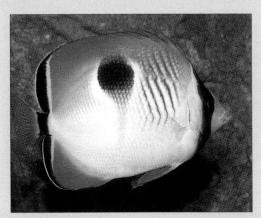

One-spot butterflyfish
(Chaetodon unimaculatus unimaculatus):
'uni' = *one*, maculatus = *spotted*.

Every species of animal and plant that has been examined and classified by scientists is given a scientific (or Latin) name. The technical term for this biological classification is taxonomy.

The scientific name is normally in two parts, the **generic** followed by the **specific**: the former is applied to the group of closely related species to which the life form belongs (the genus), while the latter identifies the particular species. The combination of generic and specific name is unique to the individual species. Examples of such names are *Elodea densa*, *Poecilia reticulata* and *Rhinecanthus aculeatus*.

Sometimes a species is divided into **subspecies**, which differ from each other but not sufficiently to be separate species. In such cases a third element is added to the first two. Examples of subspecies names are *Oreochromis niloticus niloticus* and *Oreochromis niloticus sugutae*. The first classified subspecies is called the **nominate** form, and its subspecific name is always the same as the specific. Illustrated here are two subspecies of butterflyfish.

The generic name always starts with a capital letter, the specific and subspecific with a lower case. Species and subspecies names are usually printed in a different typescript (often italics) to the surrounding text, or underlined. They are also sometimes abbreviated where the genus name has already been cited, then just its initial may be used (provided this won't cause confusion with another genus also mentioned in the same text), for example, *P. reticulata*. The specific name of nominate subspecies is also normally abbreviated: for example *O. n. niloticus.*

Scientific names may describe some feature of the life form (e.g. *caeruleus* = blue, *maculatus* = spotted, *spinosus* = spiny); where it comes from (*mexicanus* = from Mexico); or be in honour of some person connected with it, often the person who discovered it (*livingstonii* = of (Dr David) Livingstone).

Many scientific names are difficult to spell or pronounce, so many popular aquarium fishes have been given common names such as 'guppy' and 'tomato clown'. Common names are not always unique, however – there are two different 'butterfly cichlids', for example – and they are commonly restricted to one country or region, meaning nothing to people elsewhere. Scientific names are the same worldwide. It is important to know, and sometimes to use, the scientific names of your fish. If you want to research, sell, or ask someone for advice on, a species, you need to know exactly what it is.

Some fish kept in aquaria do not yet have scientific names, because there is a huge backlog of classification work waiting to be done. Many of these have been given a temporary name, indicating the presumed genus and followed by a descriptive name, often similar to a scientific specific name, but in quotation marks and normal script to show it is unofficial. An example is *Pseudotropheus* 'ornatus'.

Unfortunately some retailers are less than meticulous in their labelling, using only common names. Except where there is no doubt regarding identity, never buy anonymous fishes. The dealer may know the scientific name if you ask – if not, better to shop elsewhere.

Limespot butterflyfish
(Chaetodon unimaculatus interruptus).

TROPHIC (DIETARY) TYPES

An **omnivore** eats plants and animals.

A **piscivore** eats (mainly or exclusively) live fish.

A **herbivore** eats vegetation.

An **insectivore** feeds on insects (and, commonly, other small invertebrates) and their larvae.

A **detritivore** lives mainly on debris (animal and vegetable) found, usually, on the bottom.

A **molluscivore** eats snails and other molluscs.

A **planktonivore** feeds on plankton.

A **paedophage** lives (generally almost exclusively) on the eggs and/or fry of other fishes.

A **lepidophage** eats the scales of other fishes.

All these diets may be **obligatory** (the fish eats virtually nothing else) or **facultative** (the relevant food is taken when available or when nothing tastier is available). Obligatory feeders often have highly specialized digestive tracts and their metabolisms may be seriously affected by incorrect diet, assuming they recognize the food offered as edible at all.

3.

4.

1.

5.

2.

6.

1. Piscivore:
Pike cichlid
(Crenicichla sp.)

2. Herbivore:
Triangle cichlid
(Uaru amphicanthoides)
– pair with eggs

3. Insectivore:
Killifish
(Epiplatys fasciolatus)

4. Detritivore:
Triglachromis otostigma

5. Molluscivore:
Snail-eating doradid
(Megalodoras irwini)

6. Planktonivore:
Paddlefish
(Polyodon spathula)

OTHER DIETARY CONSIDERATIONS

Diet can present other problems. Herbivores may not eat your small fish, but they will often eat your plants (not through malice, but because they are designed to do so), sometimes voraciously reducing your beautiful underwater garden to a mass of unsightly stubble.

Some species may be difficult to feed because of highly specialized diets. You may not be able to obtain suitable invertebrates (worms, mosquito larvae) all year round. You may find it distasteful to feed live fish to an obligatory piscivore. If you can't, for whatever reason, offer a specialized feeder what it needs, don't expect it to adapt to what you are able to provide, unless you want to watch it die slowly of starvation.

PROBLEMS OF SCALE

Except in the case of fish that come from very small pools, when we accommodate them in an aquarium we are generally asking them to make do with far less space than in the wild, to forgo the ability to move elsewhere if necessary, and to live at closer quarters with other fish than is normal.

This can cause problems. Some species need private living – or breeding – space, and will commandeer part of the aquarium, driving away the other fish. If the aquarium is the same size as, or smaller than, their natural territory, they may hound their tankmates to death – not deliberate murder, but simply trying to persuade them to move elsewhere, which they cannot do in captivity, although in the wild they would just swim away. Two territorial individuals, or pairs, may turn your tank into a battleground with the other fish as innocent bystanders caught in the middle.

Always ensure that territorial species have enough space and that there is adequate room left for their tankmates – and accept that some such species require a private tank, because no aquarium is large enough to match their natural territory. While we can keep them in smaller areas, we cannot reasonably expect them to share.

Equally, remember that many species are gregarious rather than solitary, enjoying the safety in numbers provided by the shoal. It is just as unwise and unkind – albeit not so immediately disastrous – to keep shoaling fish in ones and twos, as it is to crowd those that require individual space.

The population of fishes that a freshwater aquarium can accommodate is normally calculated in terms of fish length (not including the tail) relative to surface area of the aquarium (length x breadth). For tropical fish, allow $64cm^2$ ($10in^2$) of surface area per 2.5cm (1in) of fish. For cold water fish, allow $196cm^2$ ($30in^2$) of surface area per 2.5cm (1in) of body length.

Below A shoal of small characins; many members of this group are gregarious, enjoying the safety in numbers of the shoal.

WATER:FISH RATIO

8cm (3in) 8cm

TROPICAL FISH

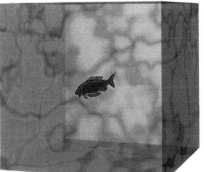

13cm (5in) 13cm

COLD WATER FISH

THE FAST AND THE SLOW

Some species are slow-moving and sedate, while others dash around the aquarium, sometimes almost continuously, sometimes in short bursts. The former may find the latter irritating, and, if they are of a nervous disposition, frightening.

The clown triggerfish (Balistoides conspicillum),
a fast-swimming reef fish.

A slow-moving freshwater discus species
(Pterophyllum aequifasciatus *var.*)

A different formula is used for marines: 2.5cm (1in) of fish per 18 litres (4 gal.) for the first six months, after which the quantity of fish can (gradually) be doubled.

These formulas relate to oxygen requirement/ availability plus anticipated filtration capability in the case of marines. Other factors such as territoriality may limit the population further. They are guidelines, not goals! Wanting to keep everything is a common urge among aquarists, but *never* overcrowd your aquarium, however great your desire to add just one more fish.

QUESTIONS TO ASK
From the above we can compile a list of questions to ask ourselves when planning an aquarium:
• What fish would I like to keep?
• How big do they grow?
• Can I provide the right size aquarium for them when full-grown?
• Am I prepared to provide the correct water conditions?
• Do they eat plants?
• Do I (really) want to grow plants?!

• What décor do these fish require?
• Will they eat, chase, or otherwise molest each other?
• Will they dig or otherwise vandalize the décor?
• Do I mind?!
• How many of each species can/should I keep?
• Am I prepared to feed them what they prefer, even if this is difficult, expensive, or distasteful?
• Do I want to breed them?
(These questions apply equally, of course, when buying additional fish for an established aquarium.)

Of necessity you may have to compromise, but only your wishes, never the welfare of the fish. Don't despair at the apparent complexity of this preliminary stage; produce a list of fish that:
a) you would like to keep
b) you think will live together amicably.
Then ask someone more expert (a good dealer, a more experienced aquarist, or the queries service of a fishkeeping magazine) to check it.

Armed with your list of fish and the answers to those questions, you are now ready to start planning the 'hardware'.

SOURCES OF INFORMATION

Books: There are a number of encyclopaedias of aquarium fish species providing basic, sometimes detailed, information. In addition there are specialist books on some major groups of fish, and on the fish of some major biotopes (including, of course, biotope information). You may not wish to buy all these, but you should be able to borrow them from your library, and some dealers keep reference copies.

Dealers: A good dealer, with a genuine interest in fish, can be an invaluable source of information. Remember that he does have a living to earn, however, so don't expect him to answer your questions at peak times; find out when his slack periods are and visit him then.

Other hobbyists: The best way to meet other aquarists is by joining a fishkeepers' club. You will be able to obtain information, and quite likely expert assistance, for example, in setting up your aquarium or in case of an emergency.

Public aquaria: Ask the technical staff for advice.

CHAPTER THREE

EQUIPMENT AND DÉCOR

In this chapter we will introduce you to the 'hardware' of fishkeeping: the equipment you will need and the decorative materials you can use to create an appropriate home for your fish.

A warning: Use only items sold specifically for aquarium use, or items which you are sure will not poison the water and your fish. Particular care is required as regards marine/brackish aquaria, because of the corrosive nature of salt water.

EQUIPMENT

TANKS

The first and most obvious item of equipment is a tank. These used to be made by fitting panes of glass into angle-iron frames, and were thus restricted to a simple box shape. Nowadays most tanks are made by sticking pieces of glass together with silicone sealant (all-glass construction). Tanks are also moulded from clear plastics, e.g. acrylic, and both this and all-glass construction have permitted greater scope in shape and size. However, some 'interesting' constructions – e.g. tall, 'thin,' multi-sided towers – are designed primarily as novelty room decorations and are, in terms of providing suitable living quarters for fish, little better than the

now universally condemned goldfish bowl. They offer little surface area and little scope for lateral movement – and few fish swim vertically! The old-fashioned rectangular glass box is far more suitable as a home for fish, and we cannot stress too heavily that this should be its main function; a tank can be decorative, entertaining and educational too, but

Powerhead

A well-maintained and decorated tank will bring you much pleasure and keep your fishes happy.

never forget that it is its occupants' entire world.

There is little wrong with using a sensibly shaped acrylic tank, but they are prone to scratching and this may detract from your viewing pleasure. The view of the interior may also be more distorted than it will be through glass. On the positive side, acrylic is durable, lighter and 17 times stronger than glass, and it is therefore less likely to crack or shatter. All-glass tanks are available 'off the shelf' in standard sizes, or can be made to order if non-standard dimensions or shapes are required. It may be cheaper to have a tank made (ask your dealer) than to buy a 'branded' one, the price of which includes transport and other overheads.

JOISTS

Joists are the load-bearing timbers under a wooden floor. It is important to site large tanks across the joists (at right angles to them), not along them. This ensures the load is distributed over as many as possible. Always site a large tank next to a wall, as the load-bearing capacity of the joists is greatest near their point of support. If in doubt seek professional advice as to the ability of the floor to carry your tank.

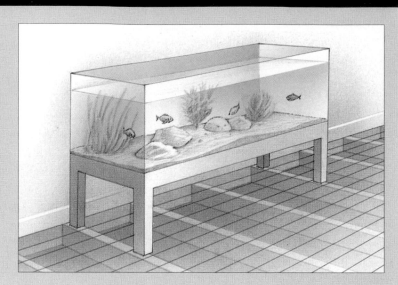

HEAVY WATER

To calculate the weight of water in an aquarium, first multiply the length x width x height of the tank to find the volume. One cubic decimetre contains one litre (1000 cc), and one litre of water weighs 1kg. One cubic foot (1728 cubic inches) contains 6.23 gal., and 1 gal. of water weighs 10 lb.

Using these formulas we find that a 60 x 30 x 30cm (24 x 12 x 12in) aquarium has a volume of 54,000cc (2 cubic feet) and contains 54 litres (12.46 gal.) weighing 54kg (124.6 lb). A 180 x 60 x 60cm (72 x 24 x 24in) aquarium – quite a common size nowadays – has 12 times the capacity and weighs well over half a ton(ne).

SIZE AND SITING OF THE AQUARIUM

In the preceding chapter we suggested that it was better to fit the aquarium to the fish rather than vice versa, but you may be limited by the space available, or by the load-bearing capacity of the floor or built-in feature on which the tank is to stand.

If space and weight are no object, a large volume of water is easier to keep biologically stable, and you can keep more fish in a large tank. If necessary you can always divide a large tank into compartments with glass or plastic 'dividers', but you can never join two small ones together. A large tank is likely to prove more versatile if your tastes change.

Although a very deep aquarium can look splendid, depth is generally less important than length and width (and thus surface area), unless you plan to keep fish with very deep bodies and/or long finnage. An aquarium more than 60cm (24in) deep may require you to strip to the waist for substrate-level maintenance, and if you want to grow plants you may find it difficult to provide lighting sufficiently bright to penetrate to the lower levels without blinding surface-dwelling fish. A depth of 40 to 45cm (15 to 18in) is suitable for most purposes.

If possible, site the aquarium where it is easily visible, but out of the way of 'through traffic' or accidental collisions with moving furniture. Avoid too secluded a site, or the fish may remain shy, and panic when approached. Position the tank at a height suited to comfortable 'viewing' from your favourite chair, ideally close to an electric socket, to avoid any need for an extension cable. Although natural lighting can be very effective, siting the aquarium in direct sunlight may cause problems with algae, and possible overheating.

You will require regular, easy access for changing water; proximity of a tap and drain may influence your choice of room, as may the age/value of the carpet – it would be unrealistic to pretend that accidents don't happen now and then.

BASES

The aquarium is normally raised to a convenient viewing level by placing it on a welded metal stand, in a smart wooden cabinet (with cupboards to house equipment), or on a built-in feature such as an alcove shelf or room-divider plinth. Occasionally tanks are set into the wall between two rooms. Home-made stands can be constructed from slotted angle iron or wood. The base must be strong enough to support the not inconsiderable weight of the aquarium when filled, and professional advice should be sought if necessary.

Aquarium cabinets are often sold with a tank fitted, and come in standard sizes, as do metal stands – so if you have a nonstandard tank specially made, don't expect to buy an off-the-shelf stand to match.

The bottom of an all-glass tank should be cushioned with expanded polystyrene (styrofoam) against any roughness or unevenness of the base. The styrofoam should be at least 1.25cm (½in) thick, and normally a baseboard of exterior or marine grade plywood (again at least 1.25cm thick) should be placed beneath it. Both the baseboard and the styrofoam are generally cut to the same size as the bottom of the tank .

HOODS AND COVER GLASSES

Hoods, like stands, come in standard sizes. You do not, however, have to buy any hood offered with your tank. Shop around to find one you like that is convenient to use. Many specialize in small plastic knobs on the access flap, which slip from damp (or even dry) fingers so that the lid closes with a bang, frightening the life out of your fish.

The purpose of the hood is to keep the occupants of the aquarium in, and extraneous matter (dirt, pets, etc.) out; it is also normally used to house one or more fluorescent lighting tubes, and may have a compartment for equipment such as fluorescent controllers and air pumps (see below).

The best hoods come complete with sliding cover glasses built in. Cover glasses prevent water from evaporating from the tank; it will condense on the underside of the glasses and drip back into the tank, preventing water loss and damp lighting electrics. In the case of marine aquaria, cover glasses will also prevent salt corrosion. You will, however, need access to the water to feed the fish, change/test water, etc., so it is desirable to have sliding cover glasses or a 'lift-out' piece. The cheap plastic condensation trays sometimes supplied are useless, as you have to remove the hood to lift the tray(s) for access, unless you 'modify' them with a craft knife!

You can have cover glasses – cheap window glass is adequate – cut by a glass merchant; they should

Above *Coral tank built into a walnut cupboard unit.*

A typical hood fitted with a fluorescent tube.

normally fit inside the aquarium rim, beneath the hood. In marine tanks, any in-tank protein skimmer is sure to protrude above the cover glasses, which will almost certainly need modification. Make sure you smooth sharp edges with emery paper before use. It isn't difficult to improvise your own sliding covers; and glass marbles, siliconed in place, make useful handles.

HEATING EQUIPMENT

The most common form of aquarium heating equipment is the combined **heater** and **thermostat** (heater/stat), available in various wattages up to 300 watts. Also available are various 'separates': internal (now rare) and external stats, internal tubular heaters, undergravel heating cables and under-tank heating mats.

Thermostats are mechanical (bi-metallic strip) or electronic; the latter usually have a sensor in the tank, while the former sense water temperature through the glass, with which they must be in close contact.

There are advantages and disadvantages to the various types of equipment:

- Heater/stats are convenient and easy to install, but heater elements tend to have a far shorter life than thermostats, so you lose 50 to 65% of your investment unnecessarily at regular intervals.
- Internal stats are more difficult to adjust, but the easier externals can be tampered with by unauthorized fingers.
- External bi-metallic-strip stats are sometimes affected by temperature conditions in the room.
- Under-tank mats reduce the amount of equipment in the tank, but once they stop working you have to replace them with internal heaters – or

TANK SIZES

Tank sizes are usually quoted as length x width x depth.

Dimensions of 'off-the-shelf' aquaria may conform to metric (m/cm) or imperial units (ft/in); the standard sizes are approximately, but not always exactly, the same. For example, the metric equivalent of 15in is 40cm (nearer 16in).

Tank sizes are sometimes quoted in terms of capacity (gal. or litres), but this doesn't take into account important factors such as surface area or horizontal living/swimming space. A 90 x 40 x 40cm (36 x 15 x 15in) aquarium has the same capacity as a 40 x 40 x 90cm (15 x 15 x 36in), but is quite different in terms of (im)practicality.

'break down' the tank to install a new mat, then start again from scratch!

• External electronic thermostats maintain the very stable temperatures which are essential to marine fishkeeping.

The heating wattage required depends on the size of the aquarium and its environment – there is a world of difference between a centrally-heated room and a cold cellar. The heating must be adequate to maintain optimum temperature on the coldest winter's night when the room heating is off. Your dealer should be able to advise you – but it is worth sitting up one cold night just to make sure.

Ideally split the required wattage between two heater/stats or sets of separates. This may cost you more in the short term, but if one stat fails 'off' or one heater element burns out, the other should keep your fish alive until you notice the temperature has dropped. If one stat fails 'on' the other will stay off, and half your heating will take a long time to cook your fish.

You will also need a **thermometer**. Various types are available: conventional tubular, liquid crystal strips, dial. They are notoriously inaccurate, so it is worth checking the tank temperature with a top quality thermometer (if you have or can borrow one), to see how inaccurate the aquarium thermometer is. (Some thermostats have temperature-setting indicators, but these are often just as bad as thermometers.)

Aquarium thermometers are cheap, so you could also buy two or three – and then take a consensus reading.

Above *A heater/stat.*

Below *The heater/stat fixed in place with suckers.*

Right *An aquarium chiller unit properly situated outdoors.*

CHILLING EQUIPMENT

In warmer countries, or during heatwaves, the aquarium temperature may have to be reduced to avoid fish losses from overheating and/or from oxygen depletion; this particularly applies to marine fishes.

Proprietary chilling units are available for use in fresh or salt water. Unfortunately, they can prove very expensive, often costing more than the livestock. A cheaper, and effective, alternative is to direct cool air from an electric fan across the surface of the water. As water evaporates, latent heat is lost to the atmosphere and the temperature drops.

FILTERS AND FILTER MEDIA

The different types of **filter** were discussed in Chapter One. It is important to buy one suitable for the size of your aquarium, number (loading) and type (environmental requirements) of fish (and plants). Air-driven UG is a good, cheap option, as it can easily be uprated by the use of powerheads if required. Remember, you can add another filter if the one you have proves inadequate, but if your filtration is too powerful then you will have to replace it, and be left with a filter you do not need and whose value has dropped because it is second-hand.

Regrettably the aquatic trade has a vested interest in selling you the largest, most powerful – and expensive – filter, so by all means ask for advice, but use common sense when deciding whether the advice is acceptable! Try requesting a demonstration in an appropriately-sized tank containing fish of the type you intend to keep.

As regards **filter media**, while expensive biological media are undoubtedly capable of supporting the vast bacterial populations claimed, ask yourself whether your fish will generate sufficient quantities of wastes to allow such a population to develop. Unless your filter volume (media capacity) is very small relative to tank size (e.g. a couple of small box filters in a 120cm/48in aquarium), it is probable that cheap media such as filter floss or foam, or just gravel, will be adequate.

LIGHTING

Nowadays aquaria are normally illuminated using one or more tubular fluorescent lights, or less commonly – and mainly for marine aquaria – mercury vapour or metal halide lamps.

Types of Lighting

Fluorescent lighting consists of two parts, the controller and the tube. The former lasts for years, the latter requires replacement from time to time, when it burns out, or, if you are growing plants, when it starts to fade. A whole host of tubes is available, producing light in various areas of the spectrum for various purposes, often at a high price. None of these tubes has, to the best of our knowledge, been proven to outshine others as regards plant growth. You should ask to see a selection in use above a tank in the shop, and choose the one whose effect you like best. Some people use two different tubes to produce light across the spectrum, an effect that can be produced using simple household tubes costing a mere fraction of the price!

Mercury vapour lamps are available in 80- or 125-watt pendant spot lamps. They can be used for both marine and (some) freshwater applications as they encourage good plant growth and exhibit the fish favourably. In addition, mercury vapour spot-lamps produce a pleasing rippling effect across the underwater scene, reminiscent of sunlight shining from above. Average bulb life is about a year, comparable to the cost of a good quality fluorescent tube. **Metal halide lamps** provide intense lighting for particularly deep tanks or where a particular wavelength requires emphasizing. Prices per unit and for replacement bulbs are very high compared to previously discussed lighting, but if light-loving marine invertebrates are to be kept, the investment may well be worthwhile. As with mercury vapour spotlamps, a pleasing rippling effect is achieved.

Arranging Lighting

The amount of lighting should be related to the aquarium occupants, both fauna and flora. Although some fish, for instance those that live near the surface in lakes and on the coral reef, spend their daylight hours in generally bright light, many others live in the shade of plants, rocks, roots and branches, or at depths where the sun's rays do not penetrate as brightly. Glaring illumination may actually damage delicate eyes as well as causing psychological discomfort. Of course, if you decorate your aquarium properly, with adequate cover for the fishes, they can make use of this shade – but then you may never see them! At the same time, remember that your plants require light to grow.

Where freshwater aquaria are concerned, if you (or rather, your fishes) do not require plants, then a single fluorescent tube the length of the tank should suffice; the fishes will not only swim around actively in this moderate lighting, but they also will show better colours. They commonly lighten their coloration under bright light, for camouflage. Brilliantly coloured coral reef fish, on the other hand, originate from a brightly lit environment, and may require several tubes to enable the viewer to fully appreciate their splendid livery.

When growing plants you may need additional tubes, and therefore to make a compromise: perhaps bright light and plants with long stems and near-surface leaves, so the fish can swim in the shade underneath; or plant one end of the aquarium with shorter plants and light it more brightly – there is nothing to stop you using one tube which is as long as the aquarium and another only half or two-thirds its length.

OTHER EQUIPMENT

Air pump: If you are using air-powered filtration, and/or a protein skimmer, then you will need a good quality, reasonably powerful air pump. Even if you have no immediate need for it, it is a useful item of equipment to have available.

Above *Fluorescent tube.*

Centre-page *Mercury vapour pendant and ballast.*

Below *A fluorescent control (ballast) unit.*

Test kits

External canister filter

Epsom salt

Peat

Airline

Air pump

Airline: This narrow bore tubing is used to transport air from the pump to the point of use.

Air valves: These are used to split the air supply between two or more outlets, and to regulate the amount of air per outlet. T-pieces and clamps can be used for the same purpose, often in conjunction.

Test kits (see also Chapter One): For freshwater aquaria you will need kits for hardness, pH, ammonia, nitrite (problems with ammonia are often linked to problems with nitrite) and nitrate. For marine aquaria, pH, ammonia and nitrite test kits are all absolutely essential. Nitrate and copper test kits will also prove useful. Freshwater test kits do not always work in salt water, and vice versa, so make sure you buy those suitable for your application. For brackish aquaria, check that the test kit in question

will function correctly in brackish conditions; if necessary, write to the manufacturer.

Water chemistry adjusters: Don't forget to buy any chemicals or materials needed to adjust your water chemistry. Always use proper marine salt for marine and brackish aquaria, never domestic (table) salt, which may contain undesirable and harmful additives. In the freshwater aquarium, however, it is acceptable to use domestic Epsom salts (magnesium sulphate) and sodium bicarbonate, and also horticultural moss (not sedge) peat, provided that it contains no additives.

Hydrometer (marine and brackish aquaria): This measures salinity. It is essential to monitor salt levels, as evaporation may lead to an increased concentration of salt in the tank, which is potentially dangerous to the fish. A hydrometer is also required when mixing up a new salt/water mix for a partial water change, to ensure that it exactly matches that of the tank. (See page 16.)

Nets: Inevitably you will need to catch a fish at some stage. It is best to have two nets, one of which you can use to guide the fish into the other. Each should be at least as large as the fish it is to be used for. Tiny nets are useless except for catching fry (and then only sometimes!), as fish elude them easily. A 10 x 15cm (4 x 6in) net is the minimum useful size.

Water changing equipment: You will need a piece of tubing about 1.25cm (0.5in) in diameter and 120 to 180cm (48 to 72in) long, for siphoning off waste water – and at least one bucket to siphon into, and for carrying clean water. Such buckets should be of 'food quality' plastic (i.e. nontoxic) and kept solely for aquarium use, under lock and key if necessary. If you need to store water before use, you will need one or more 'safe' plastic bins, e.g. those sold for home brewing.

Tip: If you are unsure about a plastic item, lick it. If the plastic has a bitter taste, don't use it. White and colourless plastics are less likely to be harmful than coloured ones.

DÉCOR

As discussed in the preceding chapter, fishes' surroundings are important to their safety in nature, and to their psychological well-being in captivity. This, and not what you think looks 'nice', must be your prime consideration. In the unlikely event that your fish ask you to match the room décor to theirs, then, and only then, will you be justified in asking them to accept blue gravel to match the curtains! The fish are an integral component of your pleasing underwater mini-world, and if they are unwell, unhappy, or dead, then décor that matches yours will be small consolation.

Unless you are reasonably confident in your geological and/or botanical knowledge, you should avoid collecting your own décor, and buy from an aquarium dealer, where you may have some legal redress if it proves unsuitable. Rocks are expensive, however, and you may find it beneficial to learn a little geology.

The aquarium décor is divided into three parts: **substrate**, **background** and '**internal décor**' such as rockwork and plants. Many people don't regard the substrate as important, and forget about the background entirely – serious errors indeed.

THE SUBSTRATE

The substrate is the term used to describe the material found on the bottom of both a biotope and an aquarium. From the point of view of the aquarist it is useful for planting vegetation and bedding rocks securely, and nicer to look at than bare glass. The fishes probably also prefer to have a substrate for this reason, and some like to move it around as a preliminary to breeding or as part of their normal feeding behaviour.

The substrate should be chosen to accord with the required water chemistry: coral sand or gravel for the reef aquarium; hardness-free gravel or sand for soft water biotopes; any nontoxic sand or gravel for hard water/brackish aquaria, perhaps with some coral sand or limestone chips added to buffer the pH.

If possible, avoid light-reflective substrates for fresh- and brackish-water fish, especially those from biotopes which typically have a dark (leaf litter) bottom. If the fish needs to dig, provide gravel it can

Artificial tufa rock

Plastic plant

Black gravel mixed with sand

Black gravel

Crushed shell

Crushed coral

River sand

Coloured gravel

Silica gravel

move, not small pebbles – and if digging or sifting is likely, avoid sharp-edged materials. This also applies for fish that rest on the bottom, or 'scan' it with delicate sensory barbels.

Artificially coloured gravels are unnatural, expensive and potentially unsafe. Although they sometimes have a plastic coating to prevent leaching of dye into the water, plastics – particularly thin coatings – do not last forever, especially if churned around by fish or immersed in acidic or salt water.

THE BACKGROUND

Most of the fish we keep are relatively small, and tend, in Nature, to remain close to the shelter of the bank or reef in order to be able to take cover and avoid being eaten. The aquarium should normally simulate an area of lake or river bank, or a part of the reef wall, not the open spaces of the main stream, lake centre, or open sea. The background is the solid vertical backdrop against which the remaining décor is displayed, i.e. it should represent the actual bank or vertical reef.

It is unkind to keep fish with bare glass on all four sides, unless the tank is large enough (unlikely in domestic aquaria) to build a central mass of rock, effectively a four-sided internal backdrop to the surrounding activity. For this reason we do not approve of the use of tanks as room dividers with the two long sides both used as viewing panels.

It is possible to buy plastic pictorial backgrounds showing roots and plants, rocks or corals. Alternatively the outside of the back of the tank can be painted, preferably a dark, bank-like colour for freshwater and brackish aquaria. Plain black is very effective, and for something less permanent than paint, use black polythene. Other possible external backgrounds include cork tiles or dark carpet, internal ones include pieces of slate. Because lava or tufa rock are relatively porous and lightweight, they are sometimes piled at the back of the marine aquarium to create a realistic representation of a reef wall.

Any internal background must be nontoxic, as must paints, varnishes or glues used.

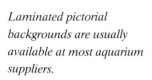

Laminated pictorial backgrounds are usually available at most aquarium suppliers.

Tank with background and substrate installed.

THE MAIN DÉCOR

This falls into two parts, the 'hard décor' (rocks, wood, coral and shells) and the 'soft' (plants).

Hard Décor

Rocks: As regards water chemistry, choice of rocks is just as important as choice of substrate. Calciferous materials – limestones (including tufa), corals and shells – should be used only in marine, brackish or hard water biotopes, not the general community, especially if its water is already hard and alkaline. Otherwise use inert rocks such as granites, gneisses, mica schists, slates and millstone grit. Regard sandstones with suspicion – a lot depends on what rocks were ground down to make the constituent sand.

Think big when designing a 'rockery', both in terms of rock size and overall effect. Nature's rockwork tends to be on a grand scale, and a good pile of large pieces will be more effective visually, and more of a home for the fish, than a small heap of large pebbles. Rocks can be glued together with silicone sealant or underwater epoxy resin for stability, but this has disadvantages if you want to move one piece or break down the tank!

Woodwork: There are several types of wood used in aquaria, the most usual being bogwood (hardened and preserved by long-term immersion in peat bogs), driftwood (from the seashore), and cork bark (from the cork oak, *Quercus suber*). All can look very effective, but each has its dangers. Bogwood and cork bark may contain – and release – tannins and brown colour. While this is fine for acid rainforest biotopes, it is not a good idea for alkaline or salt-water aquaria. Theoretically wood can be varnished to keep 'nasties' in; in reality it is virtually impossible to get varnish into all the crannies, and the surface may not 'take' it at all. Besides which, some fish like to nibble or graze on wood, and die of varnish poisoning even if the type used is safe in water. Driftwood may still contain resins, or be salt-laden, and is equally difficult to make safe.

All aquarium wood should be 'weathered', ideally by leaving it in a bucket of water in the garden for a few months. The process can be speeded up by boiling or soaking the wood in hot water. This may sound like a lot of effort, but a good piece of wood will be an asset for years, and is essential for simulating rainforest biotopes.

Bogwood

SOME TYPES OF ROCKS

Tufa Rock

Tufa rock is a porous, relatively lightweight, calcareous rock sold for use in marine and hard freshwater aquaria. Because of its weight it can easily and safely be built up into extensive aquatic 'rockeries'.

It should not be used in soft water tanks or even general communities because of its effect on hardness and pH; less well known is the fact that it is useless as a spawning substrate (e.g. for cave-dwelling cichlids) because its surfaces are too rough.

Lava Rock

This is not, as the name suggests, true volcanic rock, but a manmade byproduct of the smelting industry. It is extremely light, porous and completely inert, albeit quite expensive. It makes an ideal medium for building rock walls and is particularly suitable for the marine aquarium.

Slate

Although heavy, slate can be used to construct caves and decorative structures while also providing an excellent spawning surface for some species of fish. Slate sold for aquarium use should be completely inert and can be used in all manner of aquaria, including marine.

Limestone

Limestone may be suitable for marine and hard water aquaria owing to its calciferous nature, but in some parts of the world terrestrial limestone habitats (especially limestone 'pavement') are under threat. It is therefore recommended that this rock be used sparingly, or preferably a suitable alternative found.

OTHER HARD DÉCOR

Coral Skeletons

Real coral skeletons (dead corals) were at one time installed in every marine aquarium as standard decoration. Fortunately, concerns for conservation have lessened their popularity (their importation is banned by some countries), and synthetic coral skeletons are now being widely produced as an acceptable substitute.

Barnacle Clusters

Giant barnacles which have been vacated by their inhabitants make excellent decorations for the marine aquarium. The tiny caves provide small fish with cover and ideal places to breed.

Many aquarists use **clay plant pots** and **pipes** to create caves; such items should be specially purchased, to avoid the danger of horticultural chemical residues. Plastic pots and pipes may be toxic and are best avoided.

Above *Bogwood (far left) and driftwood are important aquarium décor items, which must be chosen and prepared with care.*

Bogwood and cork bark can be bought from aquatic retailers, cork bark is also available from florists, while driftwood you collect yourself. Empty coconut shells can make useful 'caves'.

Never be tempted to use any old piece of wood on the basis that rivers are full of rotten, dead, semi-dead, and recently living organic material – they also contain considerably more water than your aquarium, to dilute any toxins to negligible levels.

Coconut shells

Soft Décor

Aquarium plants are, for some aquarists, a hobby in themselves. We cannot hope to provide here the detail that will eventually be required if your interest develops along this path – but there are entire books devoted to the subject.

Below *Water lettuce* (Pistia stratiotes), *a floating freshwater plant.*

Plants for freshwater and brackish aquaria: You may be surprised to learn that some plants sold for aquarium use are: by nature not aquatic at all; are aquatic for only part of the year (water levels rise and fall seasonally but plants are rooted to the spot!); have the option of being wholly or partially aquatic, depending on where they happen to have taken root; or normally have only their lower parts immersed (marginal plants). *Dieffenbachia*, commonly sold for aquaria, is not only terrestrial and won't live long in water, but is actually poisonous.

You will, we trust, by now not be surprised to learn that some plants have water chemistry likes and dislikes, just like fishes, depending on the natural conditions in which they evolved. In particular, few will survive in brackish water. Plants, like fishes, can sometimes be gradually acclimatized to alien conditions by a slow process of adjustment.

Always remember that plants are living things. You wouldn't, we trust, buy a fish until you had an aquarium, or subject a tropical species to a long journey in freezing conditions without benefit of insulation. Aquatic plants are often more difficult to keep alive than fishes, so handle them with equal care. Don't buy them until the aquarium is up and running, and at working temperature for tropical species, which should be kept warm at all times.

Buying plants: Your initial choice of plants will probably be dictated not by what is 'biotope correct', or even what you want, but by what is actually available.

Most of the plants you will find offered in aquatic shops are hardy ones that will survive in a variety of water conditions. Try to buy plants that are grown rooted in special tanks or display units. Tropical plants displayed in trays may be chilled, and hence in bad condition. Plants grown in aquaria containing fish may carry disease and should, ideally, be quarantined. Look for snails in the tank – you may not want them in *your* tank, but you will most certainly get them if there are any on the plants you buy!

You may get a better choice of plants, and accompanying advice on their requirements and culture, by buying from an aquatic plant nursery, usually by mail order.

Other aquarists are another source of plants – well-rooted ones that haven't been sent by mail or left unplanted in shops for weeks. They burst into new growth with an enthusiasm not generally seen in commercial plants until months after purchase, simply because of the minimal upset. However, the warnings about disease and snails apply here too, so accept plants only from friends you trust and whose aquaria you have inspected.

Marine Vegetation: Most plants utilized in the marine aquarium are algae: not the simple 'nuisance' kind that coat underwater surfaces with a thin green or brown layer, but those better known to the man in the street as 'seaweeds'.

Occasionally a specialized tank may contain mangrove seedlings or eelgrass, but these plants can be difficult to obtain and don't usually survive long under aquarium conditions. Algae, on the other hand, are readily available from most stores with a good marine section. Those such as *Caulerpa prolifera, C. mexicana* and *C. sertularioides* will normally flourish under the correct conditions (e.g. good water quality and adequate lighting), but the chances of long-term success in a fish-only aquarium are slim. Constant browsing by fish, high dissolved waste levels and some medications all serve severely to reduce or even destroy growths of algae.

BE PREPARED

Acquire all the equipment you will need in advance; once you start setting up you won't want to have to stop because you are missing some essential item.

Remember, some of the décor goes in before some of the equipment, and vice versa, so buy both in advance – except for plants. As we have already warned, they must wait until their home is ready.

COMMON AQUARIUM PLANTS

All plants are freshwater species with the exception of numbers 1, 14, 15 (marine).
1. Eelgrass 2. Willowleaf (Hygrophila *sp.*) *3. Acorus variegatus 4. Aquatic moss 5. Java Fern* (Microsorium pteropus) *6. Hemigraphis colorata (narrow leaf) 7. Elodea densa (pond weed)* *8. Alternanthera 'lilacina' 9. Hemigraphis repanda 10. Hemigraphis colorata (broadleaf)* *11. Corkscrew* (Vallisneria *sp.*) *12. Echinodorus paniculatus 13. Hygrophila siamensis 14. Red algae 15. Caulerpa. Some of these plants, while often sold as such, are not true aquatic plants (numbers 3, 6, 9 and 10). Other true aquatics include Aponogetons, Nymphaea and water wisteria.*

CHAPTER FOUR

SETTING UP AND STOCKING A BASIC AQUARIUM

USEFUL TOOLS

A selection of useful tools and other items you may require during setting-up:

Spirit (bubble) level

Pliers

Wire strippers

Scissors

Screwdrivers

Hammer

Craft knife

Safety ruler

Cable clips

Screws

Adhesive tape

Insulation tape

Wooden or plastic spoon

Double-sided sticky pads

Silicone sealant or epoxy glue.

PRIMARY CONSIDERATIONS

Once the decision to purchase a fish tank has been made, it is easy to get carried away by the excitement, and completely disregard advance planning; and we must stress once again that planning is essential at every stage, not least when it comes to setting up, i.e. installing the tank, equipment and décor chosen earlier. It should be clear by now that buying a complete aquarium set-up and fish/plants on the same day is a recipe for disaster. The equipment will, of course, survive, but the fish will not!

This chapter is designed to lead you through setting up a basic aquarium, although everyone's set-up will be different and procedures may have to be altered to accommodate the individual. It is strongly recommended that a specific plan of action, based on these general principles, is drawn up to suit every new aquarium. Your plan should include a timetable, especially if there are glues and paints needing time to dry and/or you need to organize outside help.

Before you start, it is worth reviewing once again the suitability of your chosen site as regards viewing potential, accessibility, safety, access to electricity, water, light levels and drainage. Once the tank is installed it will be too late for second thoughts!

MAKING PREPARATIONS

It is essential, before you start, to make sure you have all the necessary aquarium equipment and all the tools required at the ready, plus any assistants you may need. Not everyone is fully conversant with electrical wiring, although most aquarium procedures are straightforward, so the help of an electrician or experienced hobbyist may be necessary, if only to demonstrate so that you can do the same job should it be necessary at a later date. Tanks are heavy items and many will require the

The aim is to produce an aquarium that will mature into a splendid underwater scene like this.

assistance of one or more fit adults to lift them. All other surplus members of the family (especially excited young children and pets) are best encouraged to go to the park, or otherwise excluded until the majority of the work is completed.

As we are dealing with water, gravel and rocks, a certain amount of mess is to be expected. Make sure carpets are protected with plastic sheeting or several layers of newspaper. That way any spillage can be quickly and effectively cleared up without permanent damage.

Dress for the occasion – glass is very dangerous stuff, so wear stout gloves and shoes when moving your aquarium, and make sure arms and legs are covered, even in hot weather.

TRANSPORTING THE TANK

A shop will sometimes deliver a large tank (plus stand and hood) to your door – and even carry it in – but most dealers will expect you to collect your goods. In these circumstances, make sure that you take plenty of blankets etc., to pack around and under the tank to avoid damage. When carrying the tank, always lift it by the base and never be tempted to hold it by the strengthening bars, which are likely to break. Ensure that it can be carried in via an uncluttered route and that it can negotiate any corners and doorways without getting stuck (the authors have known cases where a window has had to be removed and the tank passed in that way as it could not be negotiated around a corner).

Have two or more lengths of timber of approximately 5 x 5cm (2 x 2in) arranged on the floor, onto which the tank can be temporarily placed. In this way, hands can easily be slipped underneath to lift it to its final resting place once the base has been prepared.

INSTALLING AND PREPARING THE BASE

Once the aquarium stand has been positioned in the chosen spot, a spirit (bubble) level should be used to check that it is perfectly level in both directions. Large discrepancies could make the tank dangerously unstable, while a slight tilt will be noticeable as a slope to the surface of the water. Many aquarium stands have adjustable feet for such a contingency; cabinet aquaria on the other hand cannot be adjusted

and may have to be repositioned on a flatter surface or levelled with stout packing pieces.

Unless there are specific instructions to the contrary, all-glass aquaria need to be placed on a perfectly flat baseboard covered with at least a 1.25cm (0.5in) layer of styrofoam, which absorbs any irregularities in the tank base and baseboard, preventing cracking. Cut the styrofoam to fit the baseboard with a sharp craft knife and stick it to the baseboard using double-sided sticky pads. Straight edges are made by using a safety ruler – which also avoids cuts. If undertank heating is to be used, the heater mat should be laid on the polystyrene now and held in place by a few strips of adhesive tape.

FITTING THE BACKGROUND

It is generally best to measure up and fix the background when the tank is empty and before positioning it, as the task becomes increasingly difficult when the tank is against a wall, full, or you are fighting electric wires.

Plasticized 'backgrounds on a roll' are easily attached using adhesive tape. If you wish to paint the back, the glass must first be thoroughly de-greased with methylated spirits (or other 'cleaning' alcohol),

A sheet of styrofoam is placed on the chipboard base to help keep the tank level and prevent the glass from cracking.

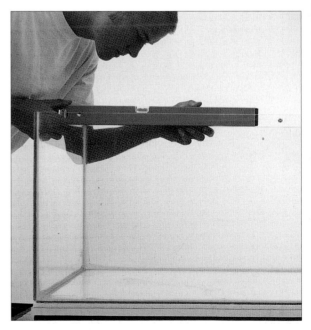

Making sure the tank is level using a spirit (bubble) level.

otherwise the paint will soon peel off. Cork tiles and other buoyant materials mounted inside the tank should be stuck into place using silicone sealant if they are not to pop up to the surface within a few days! At least 24 hours will generally be needed for paints and glues to dry, before you can proceed.

PREPARING THE INTERIOR DÉCOR

Meanwhile, the substrate and rockwork can be washed. This is a time-consuming job, but is essential if murky, polluted water is to be avoided. It also provides an opportunity to check for 'foreign bodies' that might pollute the water. Taking a few handfuls at a time, put the substrate into a sieve or bucket and wash under a running tap until clean, stirring with a wooden or plastic spoon, or hands, until the water runs clear. Rocks are best scrubbed in hot water (without soap) to get them scrupulously clean.

At this stage, decorative structures that require glueing can be constructed. Silicone sealant or underwater epoxy resin is ideal for attaching rock to rock, wood to wood, or rock to wood. Ensure that the components are completely clean and dry, otherwise they will fall apart very quickly once under water, and allow at least 24 hours' drying time before use.

SETTING UP

Carefully lift the tank into position on top of the styrofoam, making sure it is square with the base. If undergravel filtration has been chosen, the bottom of the tank should be completely covered with UG plates, assembled according to the manufacturer's instructions. Depending on the size of the tank, one or more uplifts should be fitted at this stage. As a general rule, a 60cm (24in) or smaller aquarium will require only one uplift, while a 90cm (36in) one should have an uplift in each rear corner. The larger the tank, the more uplifts are needed.

ADDING THE SUBSTRATE

Large rocks will have more stability if placed directly on the undergravel plates or tank bottom with the substrate arranged around them. In addition, digging fish can be discouraged from completely short-circuiting the filter bed by introducing a layer of pebbles at this stage.

Next the prewashed substrate can be gently poured in, making sure none fouls the seal between the tank bottom and the plate(s). The total amount of substrate necessary depends on the

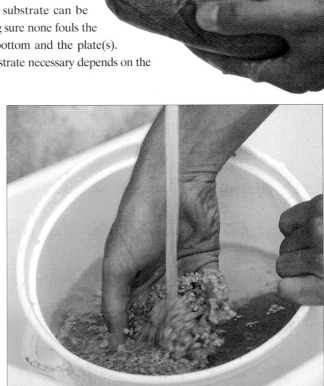

Scrub rocks only with a clean brush which is reserved for this purpose.

Fitting a section from a plasticized background roll to the outside back wall of an empty tank.

Washing the substrate in a bucket before adding it to the tank to remove any (possibly toxic) dirt it contains.

Above *Add the washed substrate, and then (***above, right***) carefully construct your terraces.*

effect the hobbyist is trying to achieve (terraced or flat), the type of plants to be used (deep or shallow-rooted), and the species of fish (diggers or mid-water swimmers). For most aquaria, a substrate depth of 5 to 7.5cm (2 to 3in) is a good starting point and can always be increased if required.

If UG is not used, plants will still require something to root in: a 2.5 to 5cm (1 to 2in) layer of substrate should suffice. If it is any deeper, there is a risk of encouraging anaerobic (without oxygen) conditions which will produce noxious gases such as hydrogen sulphide with its rotten-eggs smell!

Viewing the aquarium scene will be much more pleasant to the eye if the gravel is sloped downwards towards the front of the tank, with some terracing rocks positioned at intervals. Arrangements such as this are largely subjective and best left to the aesthetic preferences of the individual aquarist.

Don't be afraid to experiment at this stage, it can do no harm, and it will be difficult if not impossible to do so later on without severely disturbing the fish and plants.

Experience has shown that sloped gravel will tend to flatten out over a period of time if the terracing is not effective, and it is best to use larger rocks for this purpose rather than small pieces of slate which will tend to collapse.

Alternatively, rocks can be siliconed together to create a solid terrace wall.

CREATING THE UNDERWATER SCENE

Once the foundation rocks and substrate have been positioned, other forms of decorative material can be arranged, e.g. bogwood, flowerpots, slate, ceramic drainpipes, and cork bark.

If digging fish are to be housed, everything must be secured to prevent rockfalls or other toppling items falling against the glass and cracking it! Silicone sealant or underwater epoxy resin can be used to secure pieces that are a potential risk. Avoid making unstable piles of rocks from small left-over pieces – they always fall over, perhaps trapping fish, damaging plants, or even shattering the aquarium.

Bogwood and cork bark have a tendency to float until they become thoroughly waterlogged, which, under normal circumstances, may take several weeks. To enable such materials to be used immediately, they can be weighted down by attaching them to rocks using nylon fishing line or strong cotton. This sort of arrangement is easily camouflaged using plants and the like.

ROOM TO MANOEUVRE

At this stage do not overwhelm the aquarium with rockwork and other decorations. Space must be left for the addition of heaters, in-tank filters and other devices.

Plants will also appreciate room to grow and develop, and fish must have space to swim about in!

ADDING WATER

We are now ready to add water to the system. Plain, cold tap water is acceptable, pretreated to remove contaminants (e.g. nitrate, chloramine; see Chapter One) if necessary. For your first aquarium, you will probably be buying fish locally, and they will almost certainly have been kept in local tap water like yours (but check!). It is thus usually unnecessary and undesirable to modify your water chemistry at this stage, even if you wish to provide something more natural later. Once the fish are in residence, then any adjustments can be made gradually over the ensuing weeks.

Don't forget, however, that subsequent purchases will then need acclimatizing before joining the community (see quarantining, page 60).

It is possible to run a hosepipe to the aquarium and let the water gently trickle in, but a far better method is to use a plastic bucket of known volume, so that a record of the amount of water introduced can be kept to provide an accurate figure for the net water volume of the tank (part of its nominal capacity will be taken up by décor). Knowing this will prove invaluable should any medications, buffers or additives be necessary.

Add water by pouring it onto a plate, so as to avoid disturbing the substrate.

The water should not be 'dumped' into the aquarium, as this will disturb substrate and rocks alike. Instead, place a plate on the substrate and carefully pour onto that. If the water is added slowly, the gravel and rocks will have a chance to settle gradually and you can keep an eye open for potential rockfalls or (more rarely) leaks.

Once the tank is 90% full, stop adding the water and make any adjustments to rockwork or other items. Leaving a shortfall of water means that an arm can be put underwater without displacing any water onto the carpet! It also leaves space for the displacement caused by adding equipment, extra décor and bags of fish.

Note: you may have to fill the aquarium almost completely before some types of filter will function – UG outlets, for example, need to be submerged. In this case you can siphon off a little water before adding the fish.

WIRING UP

The aquarist has two main options when wiring up all the necessary equipment. Firstly, purchase a 'cable tidy' and wire everything into this single unit, which has the added advantage of on/off switches for lights etc. Secondly, a four-gang multisocket can be used to plug in each device separately. This latter method means that, should a piece of equipment fail, it will blow only its own fuse, rather than that protecting the whole system. Moreover individual items can be unplugged and then removed for maintenance without switching off everything else.

It should be noted here that various countries possess different electrical systems and standards, which may mean that these two options have their own local variants.

HEATERS

Immersion heaters are normally provided with a 'holder' – a clip with suckers – to attach them to the glass, so that water can circulate freely around them. Heaters in contact with, for example, the substrate, or which are not fully submerged, may overheat and crack their tubes. Heater/stats are best positioned at an angle of about 45 degrees and in a good flow of water. Heat rises, so this prevents the thermostat from detecting the heat from the element too soon and prematurely disconnecting, with the result that the aquarium fails to be maintained at the preset temperature. Likewise, if using 'separates', do not position in-tank heaters close to thermostat sensors. Heater/stats and external thermostats are best wired

Above *A heater placed at the recommended 45-degree angle in the aquarium.*

into a circuit without a switch, either to a cable tidy or straight to the mains. In this way, the heating cannot be switched off accidentally.

The heating system can be installed once the aquarium has been filled with water, but should not be switched on yet. Don't forget the thermometer!

LIGHTING

Fluorescent tubes are still the most popular choice for tropical freshwater tanks. Some hoods make provision for several tubes, and some have a compartment for the bulky control (ballast) unit(s), although for reasons of electrical safety these are better located beneath, or to the rear or side of, the tank. Ballast units must never be allowed to come into contact with water in any form, and this includes damp. Always make sure that they are well ventilated and cannot accidentally fall into the tank or be splashed.

Tubes are usually held in place by two metal or plastic spring (Terry) clips, screwed or bolted to the aquarium hood. If not prefitted, they are best positioned about 7.5 to 10cm (3 to 4in) from the ends of the tube. Unfortunately, plastic clips in time become very brittle and then break, allowing the tube to drop into the water. You should replace them every 9 or 12 months, or use metal ones.

The damp- (but not water-) proof cap connectors can be pushed onto the pins at the ends of the tube either before or after the tube(s) are clipped in place. Ensure that the caps are pushed on firmly and the pins located properly – otherwise the tube will not light.

Spot lamps should be specifically designed for the aquarium and not be of the ordinary household variety. They must be securely ceiling- or wall-mounted, the leads connected to a suitable electrical supply.

Lights should be wired into a switched circuit (modern ballast units usually incorporate a switch) so that they can be turned on and off as required. Alternatively, a household timeswitch can be used to switch the lights on and off automatically.

INSTALLING FILTERS

UG filters, if selected, will already have been installed, but it remains to provide the means of operation. If air is the power source, then airlines, with or without airstones, should be pushed to about 2.5cm (1in) from the bottom of the uplift tubes, and connected to a suitable air pump (see below). Alternatively, powerheads can be fitted to each uplift and connected to the mains electricity.

Following the manufacturer's instructions, assemble any external and internal **power filter(s)**, fill with the chosen media, and install as directed. Internal power filters are normally situated at the end(s) of the aquarium, with their outflow directed along its length, or towards the end/rear glass to reduce the current. The inlet and outlet of an **external canister filter** are usually sited at opposite ends of the tank, unless the outlet is to feed reverse flow UG or an above-tank trickle filter, in which case it is inserted in the uplift or fixed above the trickle tray, respectively. External canisters usually need to be filled with water before switching on the power – position the inlet tube, suck on the outlet tube to start water siphoning into the filter, then position the outlet.

Assemble any internal **box filters**, fill with media, and connect to an air pump. Box and sponge filters are normally tucked away in the rear corners of the tank.

INSTALLING AN AIR PUMP

Air pumps are commonly sited beneath the tank and the tubing run up to the top of the aquarium.

Unfortunately, when the power is off (intentionally or because of a power cut), the airline can act as a siphon, drawing water from the tank, through the air pump, and onto the floor! Avoid this by fitting an anti-siphon device between the pump outlet(s) and the device(s) supplied. If there are several of the latter, a set of gang valves will distribute the air as required.

Wire the air pump and any other electrical equipment operating biological filtration to an unswitched terminal to avoid accidental disconnection.

STARTING UP

The hood, complete with fluorescent tubes, can now be positioned and the control unit connected to the cable tidy or multisocket.

Check the wiring one last time, and if all is in order, connect the cable tidy or multisocket to the main electrical supply and switch on. As the water will be cold, the heater should now be operating and its 'on' indicator light illuminated. If not, then disconnect everything from the mains and feel the heater: it should be warm. If not, recheck the wiring. If it is correct, you should suspect a faulty piece of equipment (another good reason why livestock are not introduced at this stage!). If you have a professional electrician assisting, he will be able to test all the electric circuitry and equipment electronically, locating any problems quickly and easily.

The filtration should also be switched on to test that it works. Many aquarists, however, prefer to start their filters running permanently a day or two after the tank has been planted, to allow the plants a chance to start rooting before subjecting them to a current. The lighting can also be tested, but it is unnecessary to leave it on until the plants have been introduced.

Over the next 24 hours, the aquarium water will reach approximate operating temperature, although some fine adjustment may be necessary. Expect a range of 1 to 1.5°C (2 to 3°F) between on and off – this is perfectly acceptable. Pump and/or air flow adjustments may also prove inevitable before a perfect balance is achieved.

PLANTING

Once the aquarium water – *and* the substrate, as plants do not like having their roots chilled – has warmed up, you can buy and add your plants.

Both bare-rooted and potted plants can be gently pushed into the substrate in the required location. Do not bury the crown of the plant where the new leaves sprout but leave it just above the surface of the substrate. Some plants with stems, e.g. water wisteria, *Hygrophila*, and *Cabomba* are usually sold as unrooted cuttings, with the lower end of the stem being pushed into the substrate.

Tip: these are best planted in clumps, and long pieces can be cut into several shorter cuttings to obtain several plants for the price of one!

Decide where each plant is to go in advance, and try to resist the urge constantly to rearrange the

Above *Java Fern* (Microsorium pteropus).

Below *You do not have to remove pots before planting, but some plants grow better if you do.*

scene. Most plants respond very poorly to repeated uprooting and handling, and such treatment often kills them. This applies both now and later – plants will not spread and multiply unless their root systems are well-established and undisturbed.

It makes sense to arrange tall plants at the back and sides, with smaller plants towards the front of the tank. In this way, all specimens will be clearly visible. Obviously you will need to find out their eventual size (height and spread), ideally before purchase. In any case, avoid

Testing the water for ammonia.

over-planting at this initial stage. As the plants grow and develop, any spaces will be quickly filled, and before long you will be thinning and pruning, and looking for a suitable home for the surplus stock.

Plants need light to remain healthy, and as soon as the first specimens are planted, the aquarium lights must be left switched on for about 12 hours each day. Avoid longer periods of illumination as this will only encourage nuisance algae which will eventually spoil the whole scene.

Plants also need food. Eventually at least some of this will be provided by nitrate produced by the biological filtration, but at present your tank is devoid of such nutrients. It is thus advisable to use a proprietary aquarium plant fertilizer, at least until the tank has been matured and the fish introduced.

MATURATION

At this point, the budding aquarist will be eager to add fish, but a little more patience must be exercised before these can be added. The biological filter is as yet incapable of processing waste products, as it does not yet have a population of the necessary bacteria. If fish were introduced now, there would be an uncontrolled build-up of toxic ammonia and nitrite which would very likely kill them all. This disastrous scenario is known as '**New Tank Syndrome**'. New Tank Syndrome can be avoided by maturing the

biological filter in advance. Maturation is simply the process whereby suitable bacteria are encouraged to take up residence and breed, producing the huge population needed to process decaying matter and wastes from the fish. To achieve this, several methods can be adopted, most of which rely on supplying a food source. Decaying matter, provided by a small piece of raw meat or a daily pinch of flake food dropped into the tank, will do the job. Proprietary maturation fluids are also available, and after a course has been followed and monitored, the filters will be reliably mature. Monitoring the procedure is crucial and requires two test kits: ammonia and nitrite. By testing every day, the aquarist will notice that ammonia peaks very quickly and then slowly declines. Nitrite takes longer to build up but tends to go into a swift decline soon after peaking. Once there is no sign of either ammonia or nitrite, the tank is mature.

Maturation will require 14 to 21 days in a brand new (freshwater) set-up, and 21 to 35 days in a new saltwater set-up. This can be speeded up by introducing a few handfuls of substrate from an already mature, disease-free aquarium. Sprinkled over the undergravel bed, this will 'seed' the new aquarium with the required bacteria. Other filters can be similarly seeded with media from a mature filter.

Additionally, bacterial starter cultures can now be purchased at some aquatic stores. These claim to mature a new tank instantly, or within 24 hours, so that fish can be introduced immediately. It is still crucial to monitor ammonia and nitrite levels as some products do not live up to their claims, while others have lost their properties through being stored incorrectly. Our advice is to be patient, and use the slow, but safer, method!

It is worth noting that once a filter has been matured, it can be transferred to a new, immature aquarium, giving instant protection.

BUYING AND INTRODUCING FISH

For most hobbyists the most exciting part of setting up a new aquarium is buying and introducing the fish. Even when the filtration is mature, there is some debate as to whether you should add your fish all at once or in small batches over the ensuing weeks.

With freshwater tropicals, if the 'daily feed' maturation method has been used, all or the bulk of the population can be added at one time, provided they are fed only very lightly while the filter takes up the load. This also avoids the need for quarantining successive batches (see below). With delicate marine organisms, however, one or two at a time is the golden rule.

When deciding what fishes to buy, remember not to exceed the permissible stocking density (see page 36) of the aquarium, and, in particular, take into account the fact that many fish are sold as young specimens and will grow! All calculations must therefore be made on the *ultimate* size of the fish, *not* size when purchased. Of course, the aquarist does not have to keep purchasing fish until the maximum stocking level is reached, but may decide to cease stocking at any time to maintain a particular display community.

CHOOSING A DEALER

Visiting aquarium stores and admiring the myriad species of fish to be found there is an extremely pleasurable experience. However, if you intend to make any purchases, a slightly more careful approach is needed.

A close inspection should be made of the shop premises and the way the fish are housed. Is the store clean? Are the tanks clean? Are the tanks free of dead or diseased fish? Are the staff helpful, courteous, and knowledgeable? If the answer to all these questions is 'yes', then you can feel reasonably happy to purchase from that establishment. If not, go elsewhere!

Once a reliable and trustworthy aquatic retailer has been found, it is in your own interest to continue to give him/her the benefit of your business. After all, if you have purchased various items from numerous stores and something goes wrong, who will you turn to for help? It is not fair to ask one dealer to sort out another's mistake. The friendship of one good retailer is worth its weight in gold.

SELECTING HEALTHY FISH

If you have a particular fish in mind, look at it closely for signs of damage or disease. The fins should be intact, the eyes perfectly clear, the swimming attitude normal, respiration slow and steady, and the body free of marks, lesions, spots and sores. In addition, other fish sharing the tank must also be healthy. If any appear to be ill, disregard *all* the fish in that tank. Ignore this advice, and infection of the aquarium at home is almost guaranteed.

It may, however, be unrealistic to expect a store assistant to catch a particular individual from a large shoal of fast-moving fish (although the degree of co-operation and effort you are entitled to expect is related to the price!). But do always look carefully at those caught and bagged. Ask the assistant to 'trap' each one between net and front glass before bagging it, so you can make a final check.

Never feel obliged to accept substandard fish. After all, you are the one paying and you are entitled to value for money.

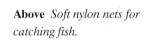

Above *Soft nylon nets for catching fish.*

Below *A fish should be carefully inspected before you net it.*

BAGGING AND TRANSPORTATION

Fishes are normally packed in clear plastic bags, often in a brown paper outer or carrier bag so that the fish cannot see out and panic at finding themselves suspended in mid-air! *Never* carry fishes home 'unshielded', unless you want them to die immediately of shock.

Some fish bags have their corners rounded so that fishes cannot get trapped and injured in the 'point'. If ordinary bags are used, it is worth asking to have

QUARANTINING

After the first batch of fish has been introduced, you should protect existing stock from diseases and infections brought in by future purchases. All too often a successful community has been decimated by disease brought in by a new fish, much to the distress of all who have an interest in the aquarium.

This can be avoided by using a quarantine tank to hold a new fish in isolation for observation over an extended period, say two to three weeks. Should it develop any disease, it can be treated and allowed to recover before being allowed into the main show tank. A quarantine/isolation tank need only be large enough to comfortably house its temporary inmate(s) but must possess fully matured biological filtration, heating, aeration, and enough decoration for shelter. Lighting is not strictly necessary but do not place the tank in a gloomy position, or the fish may be encouraged to become unnaturally shy.

Quarantining also offers an opportunity to adjust water chemistry slowly from that in which the fish was bought, to that of its ultimate home, if necessary.

You should regard a quarantine tank as an essential piece of equipment, which can, as required, double as hospital (see page 67), breeding tank (see page 75), or even jail!

Quarantining a single African jewel (Hemichromis guttatus) *in a small tank.*

bags 'cornered', i.e. the corners tied with rubber bands or taped off. A dealer who does this without your asking is a very good dealer indeed.

If you are travelling a long distance (say, over an hour), ask for the fish to be double-bagged, with oxygen. This will ensure that they arrive in good condition and not stressed by a shortage of oxygen in the travelling water. Two bags, one inside the other, will also safeguard against leaks. If you don't already have one, ask the dealer for a polystyrene fish box. Place the bags in it, packing any spaces with crumpled newspaper to avoid excessive heat loss (or overheating) and disturbance while travelling.

UNPACKING

On arriving at home, turn off the tank lights and undo the bags, then suspend them in the top of the aquarium while the water temperatures equalize. Some people may tell you to mix some aquarium water with that in the bag to avoid chemical shock,

but with freshwater fish this achieves nothing, as it takes them 24 to 72 hours to adjust to any change in water chemistry, and any major change is likely to prove fatal whatever you do at this stage. You *must* ensure that there is no such major change (see Chapter One). Try to keep stress to a minimum – the acclimatization period should be as short as possible, and the bags undone *before* they are placed in the tank (so they don't have to be taken out again).

Once the temperatures have equalized, gently upend each bag so that the fish can swim out. Make sure that they have all done so!

Most fish will swim around quite happily in their new home after leaving the bag and the lights can be switched back on after an hour or so. However, a few may be stressed enough to lie on the bottom or hide among the plants. On no account should they be disturbed by prodding or poking. Leave them in peace, with the lights out, and it is very likely that they will be fine on inspection the next morning.

Above *Float the bags of fish in the water to match water temperatures before releasing. Untying the bags first is less stressful for the fish.*

CHAPTER FIVE

MAINTENANCE AND TROUBLE-SHOOTING

GENERAL MAINTENANCE

Much of the fun in keeping fish is to be found in their regular upkeep, the essential tasks that ensure that they are kept as healthy as possible. By carrying out these tasks according to a regular timetable (such as that provided here), the aquarist can be certain that all important aspects of maintenance are covered.

WATER CHANGES

In all of the biotopes we have looked at, the water is constantly being replenished or recycled – otherwise the environment would soon stagnate and become toxic to all aquatic life. As aquarium water is 'static', it is up to you to change a certain percentage, thus reducing any nitrate build-up and replenishing minerals used up by plants and fish.

How much is 'topped up' depends on the aquarium and its occupants, but a good starting point is 25% weekly for fresh water, and 15 to 25% every two weeks for salt water. We have already seen that by measuring the amount of water introduced into the aquarium when it is first set up, we can assess the net volume; and now, using our chosen percentage, we can accurately replace the correct amount.

Siphon tube.

Used water is removed with the aid of a bucket and siphon tube (sometimes connected to a gravel cleaner). By putting one end of the tube into the tank and the other into the bucket, water can be drawn off via the siphon effect. To start the siphon simply give a quick suck on the 'bucket' end of the tube, but if you are worried about getting a mouthful of water, aquatic stores sell siphon-starting bulbs.

Pruning is an essential part of maintenance. Stems may need to be shortened and damaged leaves tidied, as here.

Algae magnets for cleaning the aquarium glass.

Replacement water may have to be prepared in advance to match the chemistry of the aquarium. Hardness, pH and temperature are important factors, as is specific gravity where marine aquaria are concerned.

Pour or siphon the new water into the aquarium, slowly and carefully so as not to disturb fish, plants, and other décor.

CLEANING FILTERS

Power (internal and external) and sponge filters will require attention on a regular basis if they are not to clog up with detritus. Any purely mechanical media can be rinsed under the tap or replaced. Chemical media such as carbon are best replaced before they become exhausted. Biologically active media, however, must be treated differently. If they are washed

THE AQUARIUM LOG

The importance of keeping an up-to-date aquarium log cannot be stressed too highly. It is a vital record of what was replaced when, test results, trends, health of the tank's inhabitants, reminders, prices etc.

By entering information on a daily basis, the whole history of a tank can be recorded and used for reference.

under the tap, chlorine and chloramine will destroy the bacteria and leave the aquarium totally unprotected. It is therefore extremely important to rinse biological media (see page 25) in aquarium water *only*. If cleaning is carried out at the same time as water changes, the old water can be used for this purpose and then discarded. *Never* rinse any media actually *in* the aquarium!

Never replace more than 50% of biological media at a time (30% is better), or the filter will have to be matured from scratch; and, if possible, clean only this percentage of media at any one time. It is wise to reduce loading (i.e. feeding) for 24 hours before and after filter maintenance.

FEEDING

The three questions most commonly asked about feeding aquarium fish are: 'What?' 'How much?' 'How often?' By now you may not be surprised to learn that the answers to these questions will vary from species to species!

WHAT TO FEED

In Chapter Two we briefly discussed some of the things fish eat in the wild, and how this affects their compatibility in captivity. In practice, unless the diet is destructive of tankmates and/or plants, it is normally easy to accommodate a variety of dietary preferences, provided the needs of each species are met. It is also important to realize that a fish's diet and the structure of its digestive system are inextricably linked, having evolved together over millennia. For example, the herbivore grazing algae from the sunlit rocks of our lake will have a very long gut, designed to slowly process the large amounts of nutrient-poor and relatively indigestible material it needs to eat to maintain energy levels. On the other hand, the piscivore lurking under a tree root in the

MAINTENANCE SCHEDULE

Note: This outline for a maintenance schedule is for guidance only, and each aquarist must devise his or her own schedule according to what proves necessary and/or desirable. When servicing equipment, always follow the manufacturer's instructions.

F = Fresh water S = Salt water

Daily
1) Check temperature (FS)
2) Check that the livestock are all present and in good health (FS)
3) Check that all electrical equipment is operating correctly (FS)
4) Feed fish, and after feeding remove any uneaten food (FS)
5) Enter observations in aquarium log (FS)
6) Dispose of protein skimmer waste (S).

Every Two Days
If necessary:
1) Clean front glass of algae (FS)
2) Top up evaporated water (FS).

Weekly
1) Test pH, ammonia, nitrite, nitrate etc. in relatively new set-ups. More often, if required (FS)
2) Where fitted, clean cover glasses (FS)
3) Add pH buffers, trace elements, and any other supplements as required (S)
4) Clean, or replace filters on powerheads, where appropriate (FS)
5) Carry out the appropriate partial water change (F).

Every Two Weeks
1) Carry out 15 to 25% water change (S)
2) Replace or clean mechanical filter media (FS)
3) Carry out pH, ammonia etc. tests in established tanks (FS)
4) Clean salt deposits from fluorescent tubes and other lighting, whilst disconnected (S).

Monthly
1) Rake through coral sand substrate and siphon off detritus (S)
2) Rake through substrate and siphon off detritus (*not* if using UG filters) (F).

Bi-monthly
1) Replace filter carbon (S)
2) Remove protein skimmer and clean internal and external surfaces (S)

3) Replace airstones in uplifts and protein skimmers (S)
4) Remove excess algae as required (S)
6) Thin out plant growth as required (F).

Every Three Months
1) Clean internal quartz sleeve of ultraviolet sterilizer, check for damage (S)
2) Clean pump impellers and check for wear (FS)
3) Use a suitable hose brush to clean out all canister filter hoses (FS)
4) Change/clean air filter pads in air pumps and check diaphragm assembly for wear (FS).

Every Six Months
1) Replace ultraviolet tubes (S)
2) Renew lighting tubes/bulbs as necessary (FS)
3) Renew or service nonreturn valves (FS)
4) Replace batteries in external thermostats with Liquid Crystal Displays (LCDs) (FS).

When Necessary
1) Clean media in biological filters (if the flow rate is reduced) (F)
2) Renew chemical filter media, e.g. carbon, peat (F)
3) Renew clogged airstones (F).

rainforest or mangrove swamp has an easily digested protein-rich diet and thus needs only a short intestine. If we offer such specialized fish the wrong type of food, then, assuming they will eat it at all, we risk compromising their health. The herbivore that is fed large amounts of unsuitable concentrated protein is likely to become obese and suffer from fatty deposits around its vital organs, while the piscivore that is offered only vegetable matter may die of malnutrition.

Never buy a fish if you are not prepared to provide for its dietary needs, and *never* try to impose your own dietary principles (e.g. vegetarianism) on any creature that is not designed for it.

Clockwise (from top left) *Brine shrimp, mysis, shrimp, shellfish and* (centre) *lancefish, are enjoyed by many piscivores and omnivores.*

PREPARED FOODS

There are many different prepared foods – flakes, pellets and granules – available, some formulated for differing dietary needs. Many are ideally suited for those indestructible 'hardy' community fishes to which we have repeatedly referred. However, a little more effort is required for fish with specialized feeding habits, especially wild fish which have no idea that a pellet is something to eat! You may need to feed them 'recognizable' food until they learn that 'what comes from the sky' is food, and in any case they are more likely to remain healthy if 'real' food forms part of their regular diet.

Even where hardy species are concerned, the thoughtful aquarist will go to a little more trouble – after all, who would want to live on nothing but 'space rations', adequate though they may be for our needs.

LIVE AND FROZEN FOODS

A number of 'natural' (though not necessarily to the species receiving them) foods are available, some of them from aquatic dealers, some requiring you to obtain them yourself. Some are also available in frozen form, but, while nutritionally excellent, lack that psychologically important 'wriggle factor'!

They include various aquatic invertebrates such as insect larvae, *Daphnia* (water fleas), *Artemia* (brine shrimp), and *Tubifex* worms, all available commercially (some you can collect or culture); and a few terrestrial ones: earthworms (home-dug), whiteworms (home-cultured), wood lice, and crickets (as sold for reptiles). There is a good possibility that our fishes encounter these or their local equivalents in the wild, as most bodies of water contain abundant aquatic invertebrates and terrestrial ones that fall or are washed in.

We strongly advise that you avoid using live *Tubifex*, as these worms frequent insanitary areas of mud and can introduce disease into the aquarium. Some sources of bloodworm (red mosquito larvae) are also suspect. Dire warnings are sometimes given regarding the possibility of introducing disease/parasites with *Daphnia* and other 'pond foods'; all we can say is that we have never had, or heard of, any actual problem of this kind. It is far more dangerous to buy a new fish!

Piscivores may need to be fed on live fish; dealers sometimes sell 'feeder' goldfish and guppies for this purpose, and many aquarists use their own or friends' surplus fry. Most piscivores can be 'weaned' onto raw dead fish from the fishmonger or supermarket.

DOMESTIC FOODS

You can use a number of domestic foods: chopped shrimp and prawn and cod roe are excellent; for vegetarians, blanched spinach and lettuce, slices of cucumber and courgette (zucchini), and cooked peas, are excellent substitutes for aquatic plants and algae.

HOW MUCH AND HOW OFTEN

This can only be learnt from research and through experience. The specialized feeders may have special requirements – some piscivores eat just one large meal every few days, while herbivores and insectivores may feed almost continuously.

Above *Pellets*

Below *Flake fish foods*

Above *Asian shark catfish* (Pangasius sutchii) *eating pellets, with tiger barbs* (Barbus tetrazona) *in the background.*

Below *A cleaner wrasse at work in the mouth of a spotted sweetlips* (Plectorhinchus chaetodontoides).

Vegetarians and insectivores are obviously more difficult to accommodate as not everyone can feed their fish every 10 minutes or so. But do think about this aspect of their behaviour, and if you can feed a 'continuous feeder' three or four times a day, then so much the better. You will probably want to feed your fish when you have time to sit and watch them enjoy their meal, but don't forget that nocturnal species also require food – after lights out.

Most people feed their fish too much. Never leave uneaten food to rot in the aquarium – there are limits to the capabilities of even the most efficient biological filter. Equally important, in the longer term watch your fishes' waistlines, especially if feeding protein-rich concentrates such as flakes and pellets. A very little of these – far less than the average fish is able and willing to consume – is adequate to maintain health and energy levels.

CLEAN-UP FISH
Some species of fish are kept as scavengers or algae-eaters. Few aquaria, however, provide the right sorts of algae at all, and none of them in sufficient quantity, to sustain even a single algae-eater.

No aquarium should provide sufficient uneaten food for a single scavenger – any leftovers should be siphoned off soon after each feed. So make sure you actually feed all your fish what they need.

TROUBLE-SHOOTING
If your aquarium has a sensible mix of fishes, properly maintained in the correct environment, and new purchases are quarantined, then it should be relatively problem-free. Even so, things may sometimes go wrong.

ILLNESSES
It is estimated that *at least* 95% of aquarium ailments are environmental rather than pathogenic, that is, the result of something the aquarist has or has not done, rather than infectious causes. Unfortunately most aquarists find this fact unpalatable and choose to convince themselves otherwise, commonly making an already bad situation worse by misusing medications; often several at once or in rapid succession, in the hope of finding a cure for the mystery 'disease'. Such chemical hotchpotches are likely to kill fish which might otherwise have recovered, or wipe out biological filtration and create an even worse environmental disaster.

If your fishes are unwell, then unless they have obvious symptoms of a pathogenic disease, assume that the problem lies in your water, and check that it is as it should be. Often all that is needed is an extra partial water change to reduce a raised nitrate level; even if the water tests as alright, it is astonishing how often a water change solves the problem.

The infective agents of some diseases, such as costiasis, bacterial fin rot, and fungus, may be present in any water but affect only fishes weakened by environmental problems. In such cases medication is required, but unless the environmental problem is remedied too, the disease is likely to recur. In addition to poor water quality, incorrect water chemistry and stress can also make fish vulnerable to illness. Prevention is the best policy.

REGULAR CHECK-UPS
Spotting any problem in its early stages may enable you to deal with it before lasting harm is done. Get to know your fishes – how each one moves, where it prefers to swim, if and where it hides, whether it sometimes rests on the bottom, how fast its gills work etc. Your prepurchase research will provide some of this information.

If you know how your fishes normally behave, then you should be able to spot any change. Check at least once a day, perhaps at feeding time, that all the fishes are 'present and correct'. But don't get paranoid about their health and start finding problems where none exist! A slightly raised respiratory rate may mean the fish has been chased – a possible problem if it happens a lot, but not a cause for instant panic. A change in colour may mean illness, but equally signify that breeding is imminent. Get to know your fish, monitor your water, and observe. You will soon learn to recognize real problems.

MEDICATIONS

Nowadays there are excellent proprietary remedies for many diseases; equally there are some which purport to cure certain conditions but may not be as effective as they claim. Where we recommend proprietary remedies, it is likely that any reputable brand will work; where we mention prescription drugs, then assume the worst about aquarium remedies. If we say there is no effective medication, then believe us! Beware of 'cure-all' medicines, and *never* use any treatment unless you are quite sure what you are treating. Random dosing in the forlorn hope of a cure is pointless and dangerous.

Always follow the manufacturer's instructions regarding dosage; *never* add a bit extra for luck, as that bit may be the difference between death for pathogens and death for fish. *Always* complete the course of treatment; some pathogens can be treated only at particular stages of their life cycle, necessitating repeated treatments over a suggested period.

Not all medications are suited for all fishes, and some are specific to fresh or salt water. Some are lethal to marine invertebrates, and many harm plants and filter bacteria. If necessary, make use of a hospital tank.

POSTMORTEM EXAMINATION

Not all fish ailments can be diagnosed by looking at the patient. Sometimes a fish will die for no apparent reason, with no specific symptoms. It is important to remember that they, like us, die of old age, premature organ failure, or cancer, and there is nothing we can do to help.

If one fish dies for no obvious reason, then, provided the water checks out as alright, the best course is to assume it was this 'inevitable' type of death.

Occasionally, however, several fish may die in mysterious circumstances, either simultaneously or over a period of days/weeks, and then you may need to ask your veterinarian to do a postmortem to establish the cause.

QUARANTINE

If you have any disease in a tank, you should impose quarantine until you have remedied it. It would be foolish to add new fishes, and unethical to sell or give away any that might be infected. Take care not to transfer the problem to other tanks; most hobbyists have the sense not to use equipment such as filters and nets on an infected then an uninfected tank, but a lot forget that buckets and siphon tubes can transfer disease, and the vast majority don't stop to think about their hands...

SIGNS OF ILLNESS

Rather than encourage 'sympathetic hypochondria' by providing a long list of diseases which you might (but probably won't) encounter, we will supply you with a list of common symptoms and likely causes (see overleaf), broken down into areas affected, e.g. fins, body, skin, plus behaviour, for ease of use. Where multiple diagnoses for a symptom are given, they are in order of probability. Note how many are primarily environmental in cause!

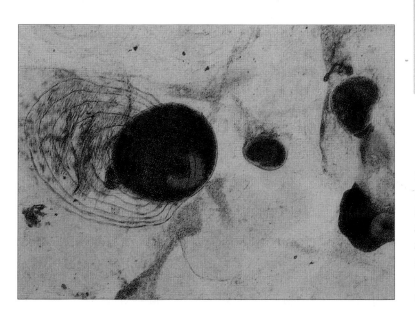

FISH DISEASES IN THE AQUARIUM AND IN NATURE

Many fish diseases, especially parasitic ones, are fatal in the aquarium if not treated immediately. This may appear paradoxical, as it is not in the interests of a parasite to kill its host, and indeed, they do not normally do so in the wild. Consider the probability of an individual tiny *Ichthyophthirius* (white spot) parasite or gill fluke finding a host fish at all in a vast body of water such as our river or lake, let alone the ocean. Enough parasites do find hosts and breed to perpetuate their species, but the host rarely acquires a lethal burden. The eggs or young parasites disperse into the water with, again, an infinitesimal chance of themselves finding a host.

In the aquarium, however, we have a small volume of water, and quite a few fish, so a very high percentage of young parasites will find a host. Just one, introduced with a new fish, can seriously infest an entire tank with its offspring in a matter of days. Unless treated, death is inevitable, usually because extensive parasite damage to the gills causes suffocation.

Left *White spot* (Ichthyophthirius) *as seen through a microscope. This disease is caused by a parasite and can be diagnosed from the appearance of pinhead white spots on the body and the gills.*

RECOGNITION AND TREATMENT OF DISEASES

AREA	SYMPTOM	DIAGNOSIS	PROBABLE CAUSE	TREATMENT
BODY	Swollen (scales protrude)	Dropsy	Water quality/ chemistry	Remedy water. No effective medication. Euthanasia if no improvement after a few days.
	Swollen (no appetite)	Digestive blockage	Unsuitable diet	½ tsp Epsom salt/ gal. may help.
	Swollen (Rift Valley cichlids)	Malawi bloat	Water quality/ chemistry or unsuitable diet	Prevention. Most bloated fish die.
	Swollen (distorted)	'Worms'	Various parasites	Piperazin or other anthelminthic from vet.
	White fluffy tufts	Fungus	Water quality, and/or injury	Improve water. Treat in 'hospital' with proprietary fungicide or 1 tsp salt/gal., or paint fungus with gentian violet.
	Pinhead white spots (and on fins)	*Ichthyophthirius* (white spot)	Parasite	Proprietary remedy.
	Grey slimy coating	Costiasis (slime disease)	Parasite and water quality	Proprietary remedy, improve water.
	Yellowish velvety coating	*Piscinoodinium* (Velvet)	Parasite	Proprietary remedy.
EYES	Swollen, sometimes cloudy	Exophthalmus	1) Water chemistry/ quality	Improve conditions, recovery may take some days.
			2) Parasite	None (very rare).
	Glazed	Poisoning	Ammonia, nitrite, inorganic toxins	Remedy cause, removing fish to safety if necessary.
GILLS	inflamed	branchiitis	1) water quality	Remedy cause.
			2) Bullying	Remove culprit.
			3) Gill parasites (rare)	Proprietary remedy.

A cichlid (Orthochromis machadoi) *exhibiting the swollen body characteristic of dropsy.*

This discus (Symphysodon aequifasciatus) *has clamped fins, cloudy eyes and darkened coloration. These symptoms are characteristic of a poor environment and stress.*

This unfortunate fish is suffering from Hexamitiasis, Exophthalmus (pop-eye), and fungus above one eye. It also has dropsy, and later died!

This fish is suffering from tail rot.

Hexamitiasis, a disease of cichlids, is parasitic but triggered by stress.

Lymphocystis, a virus disease that causes whitish cysts. It is common in 'painted' glassfish.

RECOGNITION AND TREATMENT OF DISEASES (CONT.)

AREA	SYMPTOM	DIAGNOSIS	PROBABLE CAUSE	TREATMENT
FINS	Bits missing or split/frayed	Biting/chasing	Other fish	Identify and remove culprit(s) or rehome victim.
	Edges turn grey/ white, drop off	Fin rot	Water quality	Remedy cause.
	Edges turn grey/ white, drop off, plus inflammation	Severe fin rot	Dreadful water quality!	Remedy cause, treat inflammation in 'hospital' with proprietary treatment, or paint affected part with gentian violet.
HEAD	pus-filled holes (in cichlids)	hexamitiasis	parasite and stress (water/bullying/ wrong décor etc.)	Metronidazole or di-Metronidazole (from vet) and reduce stress.
BEHAVIOUR	scratching (frequent)	skin/gill irritation	1) water chemistry/ quality	Remedy cause.
			2) Flukes (rare)	Proprietary remedy.
	Rapid breathing	Various	Many – a common symptom of illness	
	Swimming on the spot/shimmying	Toxicity	Water quality	Remedy cause.
	Loss of balance	Inflamed swim bladder	1) Water quality	Remedy cause.
			2) Internal injury	Shallow water may help. Euthanasia if no improvement.
			3) Bacterial infection	Consult vet about antibiotics.
	Gasping at surface	Oxygen shortage	1) Water quality	Remedy cause.
			2) Inadequate surface movement	Remedy cause.
	New fish die 1 to 3 days after arrival	Toxic shock	Too large a change in water chemistry or quality (nitrate)	Prevention!

EUTHANASIA

Occasionally it is necessary to put a fish out of its misery if it is past recovery or fails to respond to treatment. The most effective method is to sever the spine just behind the head with a sharp knife – death is immediate and sure. A blow to the head with a heavy object is also effective. If you cannot face the job yourself, ask the vet for assistance.

OTHER PROBLEMS

Nuisance Algae

Algae are primitive aquatic plants which tend to grow on décor and aquarium glass and are the bane of many aquarists' lives. Their growth is inevitable in the presence of water and light, so, unless you plan to do without one or both in your aquarium, it is best to simply clean them off the front glass so you can see into the tank; otherwise, consider their positive aspects, as you won't eradicate them!

Algae make rockwork look more natural; they may grow on higher plants, but generally only on old, dying leaves. Problems arise only if those are the *only* leaves (a healthy plant constantly grows young foliage to replace the old). Algae remove nitrate from the water, and, if rampant, warn that levels may be rising. Finally, they harbour micro-organisms that are excellent first foods for fry.

Equipment Failure

Keep a spare heater/stat and air pump diaphragm, and replace them if you use them! Filter motors sometimes burn out, tanks sometimes break, often at inconvenient times when shops are shut.

You should always have a contingency plan for such crises, whether it involves throwing yourself on the mercy of your friends, asking your dealer if you can wake him at 03:00 in an emergency, or using the bath tub!

Power Outages

Don't panic! Report the problem, and ask for an estimate of duration. Even in cold weather serious problems are unlikely, provided the power returns within a couple of hours.

If the outage is likely to be longer, immediately cover the tank with insulating material such as blankets. Emergency heaters can be improvised from plastic bottles or clear plastic bags full of hot water (e.g. from the domestic cylinder or a gas kettle), stood or suspended in the tank.

To provide oxygen – for fish and filters – connect a bicycle/car tyre or inflatable mattress pump to the aeration system and pump for five minutes every hour. If you have none of these, blow down the tubing – your breath may be rich in carbon dioxide, but it will activate any airlifts and agitate the surface.

There is nothing you can do to keep power filters 'alive', so look out for signs of ammonia and nitrite toxicity after any major outage. Reduce loading by stopping feeding, and keep changing water to dilute toxins while the filter regenerates. If necessary use zeolite to remove ammonia.

For one-tank households, a number of battery-operated heaters and air pumps are available. Aquarists with several tanks, and who are subject to frequent outages, may wish to consider purchasing a generator.

Opposite *Jewel cichlid* (Hemichromis guttatus) *with three-day-old fry. The arrival of fry is a sure sign of a healthy tank.*

Below *Hair and other algae.*

CHAPTER SIX

BREEDING AQUARIUM FISH

The prime instinct of all creatures is survival; not just of the individual, but also, through reproduction, of the species – and the urge to breed is very strong indeed. It should thus come as no surprise to discover that many fish can be induced to breed in captivity, some requiring little if any persuasion. It might equally be said that it is unfair to prevent – whether intentionally or through ignorance – the fulfilment of the breeding instinct, although considerations of tank space and behaviour make captive breeding next to impossible in some species. Nevertheless, enforced celibacy should be avoided where practicable, even if there is no desire to rear the fry. In the community aquarium most will be eaten, but the parents will at least be able to fulfil their urge to spawn, and the aquarist will have the pleasure of watching the spectacle and knowing his or her fish are 'happy'.

BREEDING STRATEGIES

Nature has evolved countless different breeding strategies among fish, far too many to detail here. They can, however, be divided into a few major categories. Firstly, while most species produce eggs which are fertilized and hatch externally (egglayers),

a number are fertilized internally and give birth to fully-formed young (livebearers or viviparous fishes). There is a further major distinction between species that practise parental care and those that don't. In the case of the former, brood care may be by one or both parents, and involve simple guarding or more complex mechanisms such as taking the

Above *Three-day-old* Ancistrus temminckii *fry – a herbivore that browses on algae.*

A female Astatotilapia – *formerly* Haplochromis – burtoni *with newly released young.*

eggs into the mouth for protection (mouthbrooding). There are almost as many minor variations on these major themes as there are species.

Not surprisingly, breeding strategies commonly reflect conditions in the natural habitat. After all, it makes sense to use what is advantageous in the biotope to counteract its hostile elements, whether or not brood care is practised. Thus species from densely vegetated habitats commonly attach their eggs to plants, or at least scatter them among this cover. Where there are numerous bottom-dwelling predators, eggs are attached to substrates near the surface. Those species which themselves find shelter among rocks often conceal their eggs there, while on the coral reef, anemone fish tend their eggs under the protection of the tentacles of their host. The majority of reef fish, however, are eggscatterers, whose eggs, and subsequently fry, become part of the plankton.

The eggs themselves sometimes reflect their natural environment. They may use colour, or lack of it, for camouflage. They may be numerous, reflecting the degree of danger to themselves or to the resulting fry. Then again, some fishes that live in rapids produce a few very large eggs, and hence large fry that stand a better chance of survival in the current. Mouthbrooders likewise tend to produce relatively few large eggs and fry.

Eggs may be **adhesive**, for attaching to cover, or **nonadhesive**, for scattering into the current or on the substrate, picking up for brooding, or moving from one hiding place to another. Some can even withstand lack of water, and, indeed, require this treatment before they will hatch. These belong to fish from temporary pools which dry up on a regular basis. The adults perish, but their eggs remain in the dried-out debris or mud on the bottom, hatching when the rains come. Even more remarkably, they may not all hatch at the first hint of water; some require two or more wettings to stir them into action – a safeguard against brief wet spells too short to permit young fish to mature and breed in their turn.

A bubblenest.

THE IMPORTANCE OF NATURAL CONDITIONS

If fish are vulnerable to unsuitable water conditions, how much more likely that delicate structures such as eggs and sperm will succumb. Even species acclimatized to a variety of aquarium conditions commonly require simulation of their native water to produce and fertilize viable eggs.

Perhaps less obvious is the fact that many species require their environment as a whole to resemble that in which they evolved. This applies particularly to those that tend their eggs and for whom breeding is a relatively long-term commitment rather than a five-minute fling among the *Cabomba*. A rainforest species that spawns on surface vegetation is hardly likely to perform in a plant-free aquarium, any more than a lake-dwelling crevice-spawner with no rocks or substitute caves. Those are rather obvious examples, but what of species that have a deep-seated need to move substrate as part of their breeding ritual, but whose mouths are too small to shift the gravel provided by their owner? That is easily remedied – once you know what the problem is. But accommodating mud-tunnellers or crater-nest builders (such nests can be almost 1m/3ft in diameter and 30+cm/over 1ft high) can be more of a challenge.

Some problems with 'difficult' species, and in particular marines, have yet to be solved, or in some cases identified, so don't expect to find all the answers when you research a species – it may be you who first works out what is required. As ever, the obvious place to look is in the natural habitat, and the species' relationship to its biotope. It may require a change in temperature, a special diet, even the presence of some other organism, e.g. an anemone for marine clownfishes or a mouthbrooding cichlid to parasitize for the cuckoo catfish (*Synodontis multipunctatus*).

Breeding Coral Fishes

This is one area which remains a major challenge for the amateur. A few species have been successfully spawned, but it has proved difficult to produce sufficient micro-organisms, capable of surviving in salt water, as a substitute for the plankton on which the fry would feed in the wild.

Some coral fish are now being bred commercially in tropical coastal areas, using natural sea water (sometimes on a constant exchange basis) to maintain

CAPTIVE BREEDING AND CONSERVATION

Many millions of ornamental fish are kept in captivity all over the world, and the demand for new stock is constant. If it were necessary to obtain all the required stock from the wild, then many species would soon be endangered, if not extinct.

Luckily, many of the most popular freshwater species are now bred commercially in numbers adequate to meet demand, so the problem of conservation doesn't arise. Others, however, are normally bred – if at all – only by amateurs, who thus have an important role to play in preventing depletion of wild stocks. In a few cases, aquarists are actually participating in captive breeding programmes for species which are endangered or already extinct in the wild (not necessarily through any fault of the aquarium trade). It has to be said, however, that it is perhaps over-optimistic to assume that these captive-bred fish can be used for restocking, as they would probably be unable to cope with the inimical wild habitat after the security of the aquarium. Still, who knows? Nevertheless, the emphasis must be on breeding to prevent depletion of wild stocks rather than to remedy it.

The situation is somewhat different with **marine fishes**, where successful captive breeding by hobbyists remains a rare event. However, huge strides forward have been taken in recent years as regards the commercial breeding of some species. Nevertheless, it is essential that wild populations are conserved by sensible restrictions on numbers collected and insistence on nondestructive and discriminating methods, i.e. individual capture by net.

Deformed fish like this should never be used for breeding.

optimum conditions and provide a natural food supply for the fry.

Hopefully, in the years to come, more will be learned and greater success achieved in breeding fish in the marine aquarium. At present, however, breeding remains very much the province of the freshwater aquarist.

SELECTION OF BREEDING STOCK
In the wild, natural selection ensures that in general only those individuals most suited to their environment survive and breed – 'survival of the fittest'. Survival in the aquarium is a very different and much easier affair (provided the aquarist is competent), and this, coupled with failure to select top quality breeding stock, has resulted in many long-term aquarium-bred species becoming feeble shadows of their splendid wild ancestors. In particular the tendency of hobbyists to mate brothers and sisters indiscriminately can have alarming consequences such as loss of size and colour, physical deformity, cancers, blindness and loss of vigour.

It is important always to obtain unrelated stock if possible (by buying tank-breds from two or three sources), and to select only healthy, lively individuals which resemble wild fishes as closely as possible in appearance and behaviour. If necessary, wild stock can be used to 'revive' tank-bred lines by introducing genes still honed by natural selection.

COMMUNITY OR BREEDING TANK?
Whether or not you wish to breed your fish and rear fry, you should be aware of what to expect if they pre-empt you in this matter.

In particular, species practising parental care may be disruptive, defending a (potential) breeding territory against their tankmates. On the credit side, such 'parental' species often rear a brood with little or no assistance from their owner. Where there is no parental care, however, the aquarist must rescue the eggs before they are eaten by tankmates – or the parents! This is clearly impracticable if the tiny, usually transparent and often almost invisible, eggs are scattered the length and breadth of the decorated community aquarium, so it is normal to transfer breeding stock (a pair or small group, depending on species) to a separate tank, specially equipped for spawning the species in question. Disruptive parental breeders, such as cichlids, are also sometimes moved to private tanks (or isolated within a large tank, using a divider). The quarantine/hospital/prison tank can be used, provided it is large enough. It may, however, not be large enough to rear the fry to saleable size, so if you find you enjoy breeding fish, you will need at least one extra good-sized aquarium.

ARTIFICIAL BREEDING TECHNIQUES FOR
NON-PARENTAL SPECIES

Eggscatterers (nonadhesive) e.g. danios, small barbs: A piece of fine plastic mesh (such as that sold for shading greenhouses) can be draped from the tank rim to form an open-topped cage in the otherwise bare tank. The fishes are placed in this cage, and their eggs fall through the mesh to safety. The parents are removed after spawning (as for all the following egglayer techniques).

An alternative is to place a layer of glass marbles on the bare bottom of the aquarium; the eggs fall through the interstices. It may be necessary to lower the water level to reduce the 'drop', during which the eggs are vulnerable to predation.

For species which require the psychological security of vegetation, Java moss (*Vesicularia dubayana*) can be used instead of, or as well as, marbles. After spawning, the marbles and/or moss are removed (the latter should be shaken around in the water to wash out any eggs lodged in it).

Eggscatterers (adhesive) e.g. tetras: A large amount of Java moss is placed in the tank, or alternatively it can be planted with fine- or small-leaved plants such as *Myriophyllum*, *Cabomba* and *Hygrophila*. Prunings of these plants from the community tank can be used to good effect, and need not even be planted; once the eggs have hatched they can be discarded. The adults make spawning runs through the plants, scattering eggs which stick to the vegetation.

Plantspawners (e.g. rainbowfishes and some killifishes): These fishes deliberately attach their eggs to vegetation instead of scattering them. Real plants can be used, but do not always take kindly to being moved around from tank to tank, nor to some aspects of the artificial hatching process.

Instead use spawning mops, which are easily made from strands of nylon 'wool' tied to corks to create floating 'vegetation', or pebbles for bottom-spawners. Use lengths of wool about 15 to 20cm (6 to 8in) long, doubled over and secured to the cork/pebble at their centre. Some species prefer green wool! Spawning mops can be used in the community aquarium and removed for hatching elsewhere.

Annual killifishes: The bottom is covered with peat, into which the fish dive during their spawning embrace. After spawning, the water is drained off and the peat squeezed free of excess moisture before being stored in plastic bags or boxes.

The storage period varies from species to species, so it is important to label the container with the species name – and the date!

Livebearers: These fish commonly join their tank-mates in eating their young, though a few generally survive in well-planted tanks.

Heavily gravid females can be placed in a breeding tank in breeding traps: specially designed plastic containers with perforations through which the newly-born fry can escape from their mother.

Below *A single egg of* Chilatherina bleheri *adhering to a strand of a spawning mop.*

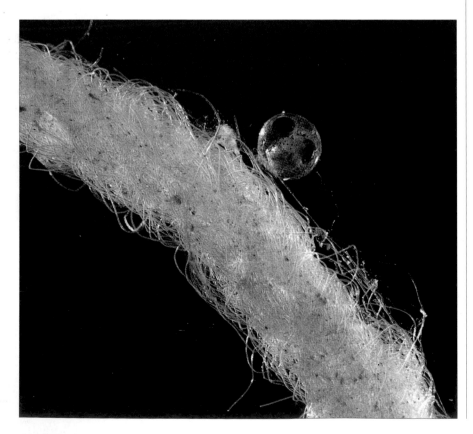

HATCHING

Eggs are normally hatched in the water in which they were laid (or water of equivalent chemistry for stored killifish eggs), although they are sometimes moved to a smaller container, floated in an aquarium for warmth.

Gentle aeration is required to draw oxygenated water over the eggs without churning them around.

Chemicals are sometimes added to prevent attack by bacteria or fungus – some of these, for example methylene blue, are harmful to plants and filter bacteria.

REARING

Fry vary in size, and hence so must the first foods they are offered. In general live foods are necessary initially to trigger the feeding response, and these may range from infusorians (micro-organisms) through microworm and newly hatched brine shrimp to *Cyclops* and small *Daphnia*. Later fry can be weaned onto cod roe, crumbled flake and small granules. Fry are generally omnivorous – specializations develop nearer adulthood.

Successful rearing requires considerable attention to tank hygiene – especially if the young fish are fed heavily to promote growth. They are usually more susceptible than adults to incorrect water chemistry, poor water quality and sudden environmental changes. It is also important that they have adequate space or their growth may be retarded.

CULLING

It is generally impracticable to rear all of the hundreds, sometimes thousands, of fry resulting from a single spawning, and their numbers need to be reduced by culling. It is much better to rear a few good quality youngsters than a mass of inferior ones.

In the case of large broods, it is common to reduce numbers to manageable proportions by siphoning off a portion of the brood immediately after hatching; the easiest, and most natural, method of disposing of them is to feed them to your other fish. Further culling may be necessary later, to reduce numbers further or eliminate runts and deformed specimens.

Beware of culling simply on a size basis, as in some species size differences between the sexes manifest at an early age, and you could end up with all one sex.

To avoid disappointment and problems later on, research your market before rearing any fry; there is no point in producing a large batch which you cannot sell. You are unlikely ever to make your fortune from your fry (and enjoyment should be the primary consideration), but if you select saleable species for breeding – those for which there is a demand not satisfied by the large commercial breeders – then you should be able to make your hobby at least partially self-supporting and do your bit for conservation at the same time.

Above left and right *Siamese fighting fish* (Betta splendens) *spawning sequence.*

LINE BREEDING

Line breeding is the carefully planned mating of selected individuals in order to produce or enhance some desirable feature e.g. developed finnage, as in the guppy (*Poecilia reticulata*); or to make permanent some characteristic that has appeared by chance e.g. colour mutations like the marbled form of the freshwater angelfish (*Pterophyllum scalare*), below.

CHAPTER SEVEN

THE MAIN GROUPS OF AQUARIUM FISH

The total number of species of fish accessible to the aquarist nowadays numbers well into four figures, and with hundreds generally available it is impracticable to provide details of each in any general handbook on fishkeeping. Instead we present here an overview of some of the main groups of aquarium fishes, both freshwater and marine, so that the reader may acquire some idea of their general habits and requirements.

Comprehensive catalogues of aquarium fishes are available, and the better aquatic dealers commonly keep copies on their shelves. Reference to these, or to specialist publications on different groups of fishes, is advisable before making any purchase. The sheer diversity of size, habits and other features mentioned *within* some groups will, we trust, reinforce our repeated admonition that each and every unfamiliar species must be researched.

Above *Seahorse* (Hippocampus *sp.*).

Below *Blue dolphin cichlid* (Cyrtocara moorii).

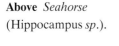

FRESHWATER GROUPS

Representatives of all the groups listed here, and indeed, of individual families and genera within those groups, are found in a number of extremely diverse biotopes, and thus may require quite different treatment in captivity. We have endeavoured to summarize here the major points that apply to each group in general.

CHARACINS

The characins are a huge group of tropical species from South and Central America, and Africa, and include many very popular small- to medium-sized

A selection of Lake Malawi cichlids.

aquarium fishes – tetras (family Characidae), hatchetfish (Gasteropelecidae), pencilfish (Lebiasinidae), and headstanders (Anostomidae) – as well as the larger piranhas (also Characidae). Between them they encompass a size range of 2 to 100+cm (¾ to 40+in) and virtually the entire dietary gamut, including aquarium plants and each other. Most characins originate in soft acid water, although many have been acclimated to hard alkaline conditions. **Tetras** are generally found in shoals in slow-moving or still open water, near vegetation and tangles of roots and branches, to which they can retire if threatened. **Hatchetfish** enjoy similar conditions but live at the surface, and are able to 'fly' out of the water to escape predation. **Pencilfish** are also surface dwellers, hanging motionless like

SMALL FRESHWATER GROUPS

In addition to the main freshwater assemblages listed, there are a number of smaller groups of varying suitability for the aquarium. **Rainbowfish** (Melanotaenidae) are small, colourful, peaceful fishes from Australasia, eminently suited to community life. **Leaf fish** and **nandids** (Nandidae), by contrast, are small and generally highly predatory. **Snakeheads** (Channidae) are large and predatory but, like large cichlids, can make excellent pets given a tank of their own. **Arawanas** (Osteoglossidae) are sometimes seen for sale, but are difficult and likely to outgrow their quarters. They are best left in the shop, if only for conservation reasons. **Elephantnoses**

(Mormyridae) are commonly seen, but delicate. They need a fine, soft substrate in which to delve with their sensitive snouts, and are crepuscular (active at twilight) in their habits. **Spiny eels** (Mastacembelidae) are similar in their requirements. **Knifefish** (Apteronotidae, Notopteridae) can grow large (to 60cm; 24in) and are chiefly nocturnal. **Butterflyfish** (Pantodontidae) are rather delicate, elegant surface-dwellers suited to a peaceful community.

With the exception of the rainbowfish, these small groups are all probably better suited to the experienced or specialist aquarist.

Campylomormyrus rhynchophorus, *an elephantnose*

Rainbowfish Melanotaenia trifasciata (above) *and* Melanotaenia boesemani

Channa argus, *a snakehead species*

Mastacembelus erythrotaenia, a *spiny eel species*

South American knifefish (Eigenmannia virescens)

Butterflyfish (Pantodon buchholtzi)

CHARACINS (cont.)

bits of twig during the day and becoming active at dusk. **Headstanders**, by contrast, come from a quite different biotope – fast-flowing water with rocks, in whose vertical cracks they find shelter – and are thus less suited to the general community.

All characins are eggscatterers, and only a few of them practise any form of parental care.

SPECIAL CONSIDERATIONS IN CAPTIVITY

Many species show better colour under the correct water conditions, which are almost invariably necessary for breeding. Shoaling species should be kept in groups of at least six, as they will be stressed without the psychological security of the shoal. A combination of adequate cover and plenty of swimming space is also required by all but the largest species.

Small characins are often eaten by larger tankmates, even non-piscivores – the temptation of a moving, bite-sized 'snack' is irresistible. The problem rarely occurs in a new community of young, small fishes, but is common when an elderly tetra dies and is unthinkingly replaced with a new one which is small in relation to its older tankmates!

Hatchetfish are particularly sensitive to poor water quality and incorrect chemistry, and are also likely to jump out if frightened, so a tight-fitting cover is required to prevent losses. A childproof cover is necessary for flesh-eating piranhas, and every care must always be taken when dealing with these fishes: they are quite unpredictable and their teeth can cause serious injury.

Breeding: Even given correct water conditions, breeding is not simple. Spawning is easy to promote, but few species practise brood care and the untended eggs are generally eaten by tankmates – or the parents! In most cases it is necessary to use a separate, well-planted breeding tank, from which the adults are removed after spawning so that the eggs can hatch unmolested.

Top Piaractus brachypomus
Above Semiprochilodus taeniurus, *a South American characin*
Above left *Piranha* (Serrasalmus nattereri)
Left *Tetras* (clockwise from top left): *Congo tetra* (Phenacogrammus interruptus), *Penguin fish* (Thayeria boehlkei), Paracheirodon axelrodi, Petitella georgiae, Hyphessobrycon griemi, *and* (middle), Hyphessobrycon callistus callistus).

CYPRINIDS

This group is native to tropical and temperate zones, with representatives in Europe, southern North America, Asia and Africa, occurring in a variety of habitats and water conditions. It includes not only popular tropical aquarium fishes such as rasboras, barbs, danios and 'sharks' (all family Cyprinidae), and loaches (Balitoridae and Cobitidae), but also goldfish and carp.

Some, e.g. loaches, and to a lesser extent 'sharks', are bottom-orientated, but the majority prefer open areas (with adjacent plant cover) in the mid-water zone, and thus have similar habitat requirements to small characins, with which they generally mix well in captivity. Again, like small characins, many prefer to live in shoals.

Sizes range from 2cm (¾in) to 70cm (30in) or more. The smaller species are often, but not always, omnivores or insectivores, while some of the larger ones are herbivores.

As with other groups, size, habits and/or requirements make some unsuitable for the community aquarium, or, indeed any aquarium – all but the smallest carp, even the ornamental types, do require the swimming space offered them by a pond.

Cyprinids are eggscatterers, commonly spawning on or in among vegetation.

SPECIAL CONSIDERATIONS IN CAPTIVITY

Much of what applies to tetras is also valid for the small open-water cyprinids, except that they are generally 'hardier' and many do not require, or appreciate, soft acid water. Some loaches also benefit from being kept in groups, while others, and the 'sharks', can be territorial, squabbling among themselves and harassing other fishes. The Chinese algae eater or sucking loach (*Gyrinocheilus aymonieri*) is notorious for attaching itself to large, flat-sided fishes and feeding on their body mucus.

In addition, some of the small barbs have a deserved reputation for nipping the fins of other fishes, but this can often be remedied by keeping them in a shoal.

Above *Zebra danio* (Brachydanio rerio)
Below *Harlequin rasbora* (Rasbora heteromorpha)

Breeding: As with most characins, parental care is unknown, so although eggs are commonly laid in the general community, intervention by the aquarist is necessary to produce fry. Plantspawners will require a well-planted breeding tank, while a substrate of marbles or Java moss should be used for eggscatterers (see page 76).

Below left *Black-banded Osteochilus* (Osteochilus vittatus)
Below right *Two-spot barb* (Barbus bimaculatus)

CATFISH

Catfish (order Siluriformes) take their name from the whisker-like barbels around their mouths. The barbels are delicate and extremely sensitive organs of 'taste' used to help find food, and are particularly useful for the many species that are nocturnal or lurk in dark or shady places. Catfish differ from most fish in that they are protected by thick skin or bony plates (scutes) instead of the usual scales. Some have mouths modified into suckers. They form an extremely large, diverse and widespread group (comprising 32 families) found all over the world and in salt as well as fresh water, although the majority are found in tropical freshwater biotopes of all types. Most catfish are bottom-dwellers.

The size range of catfish almost matches their geographical range: from a diminutive 2.5cm (1in) to 2.4m (8ft) or more. The largest are formidable predators, preying on snakes, frogs, toads, aquatic birds, and mammals, as well as other fishes. As is to be expected of such a large and varied group, however, all dietary types are included.

All are egglayers, with a diversity of breeding habits commensurate with the vast number of species. Some are known to practise parental care, but because most catfish are difficult to breed in captivity, their breeding habits are often unknown. One species substitutes its eggs for those of spawning mouthbrooding cichlids, and is thus an aquatic 'cuckoo' – a fact that was discovered only by chance, by aquarists.

Above Synodontis angelicus, *an African catfish.*

SPECIAL CONSIDERATIONS IN CAPTIVITY

The delicate barbels of bottom-dwelling species may be damaged by coarse substrates, leading to serious problems with bacterial and/or fungal infections; moreover, species with long barbels require careful handling. Equally the robust, sharp, dorsal and pectoral fin spines can become entangled in nets, and puncture both polythene bags and unwary aquarists.

Some very large species are delightful as youngsters and are often purchased by aquarists who do not realize the eventual size of these giants. Even those who are aware of this problem fail to realize the impossibility of housing their pet, when adult, in a domestic aquarium – and the zoos are already overwhelmed with outsize catfish who have outgrown their welcome in the living-rooms of suburbia.

Catfish have a long-standing reputation as aquarium scavengers, but in practice the majority require proper feeding (with a suitable diet at an appropriate time of day – or night), instead of the semi-starvation commonly inflicted on them through ignorance. Some of the suckermouth varieties may attach themselves to large, flat-sided tankmates and feed on their body mucus, causing physical and psychological damage.

Some species will gnaw wood if it is available, and are likely to be poisoned if the wood is varnished.

Breeding: It is necessary to research the breeding habits (if known) and aquarium techniques for individual species, or at least genera. Success is most likely in egg-guarding species such as *Ancistrus.*

Above left Arius jordani, *an Australian catfish.*
Left Panaque nigrolineatus, *a South American catfish.*

CYPRINODONTS (TOOTHCARPS)

The cyprinodonts can be divided into two distinct main subgroups. The **livebearing toothcarps** (family Poeciliidae) include some very popular, hardy, and easy to keep and breed types such as guppies, platies, swordtails and mollies. Of the **egglaying toothcarps** or **killifishes** (Cyprinodontidae), many are regarded as tricky if not difficult, and strictly for the specialist.

Generations of careful selective breeding have produced fancy strains of some livebearers, and the original wild forms are now rarely – if ever – seen in captivity.

The group as a whole is largely tropical, with representatives in the Americas, Africa and Asia, while a few species are native to more temperate zones. In general, the livebearers are found in hard, sometimes brackish water, and the egglayers commonly in soft acid conditions, but there are exceptions.

Size ranges from 2cm (¾in) to 24cm (9.5in), so there are no monsters to beware of in this group, although some are, nevertheless, predatory. Most feed on insects, however, and some on vegetation, in the wild. Killies generally remain close to the water's surface, many having a flattened upper head and upward-opening mouth, allowing them to cruise just below the surface and snap up anything edible on it. Livebearers commonly venture into mid-water as well.

Some 'killies' are what is termed annual fishes. These live very short lives in temporary pools, leaving their eggs to survive the drying up of the habitat and produce a new generation when the rains next come.

Nothobranchius rachovii, *a killifish*

SPECIAL CONSIDERATIONS IN CAPTIVITY

Most livebearers will take, and thrive on, dried foods, but many killifishes require live or frozen live foods.

Like many other surface-dwelling fishes, a primary escape mechanism of toothcarps is to jump from the water – and, if it lacks a close-fitting cover, out of the tank. In fact killies (especially the rarer, more expensive ones) have an uncanny ability to find the tiniest gap and commit suicide on the carpet.

The annual species are very shortlived – though generally not so much so as in the wild – and, since they are normally offered for sale only as well-coloured adults, may die of 'old age' soon after purchase. However, their eggs, being able to withstand lack of water, can be sent from enthusiast to enthusiast by post in plastic bags of moist peat, and this is probably the best method of obtaining stock. [**Publishers note:** be aware that in some countries it is illegal to send fishes or fish eggs across provincial, state or international boundaries without a permit.]

Breeding: It is virtually impossible to avoid breeding livebearers, but they are liable to eat their own fry as soon as these are born, unless a breeding trap is used (see page 76). Considerable care and attention to stock selection is required, however, to produce 'pedigree' strains, and this has become almost a hobby in itself.

Breeding killifish, annual and otherwise, requires considerable intervention by the aquarist. In general small breeding tanks are used, with spawning mops for non-annual plant-spawners and a substrate of loose peat for annual bottom-spawners. The eggs of the former group are normally hatched immediately in small containers, while the latter have to be dried out, stored in a warm place, then wetted weeks, or sometimes months, later to simulate the onset of the rains: fiddly, but great fun!

Nothobranchius patrizii

Poecilia nigrofasciata

Green swordtails (Xiphophorus helleri)

Amidiochromis compressiceps,
a Lake Victoria cichlid.

Pelvicachromis taeniatus,
a West African dwarf cichlid.

Cyphotilapia frontosa,
a Lake Tanganyika cichlid.

CICHLIDS

Members of the cichlid family (Cichlidae) are found chiefly in tropical Africa and America, with a small handful of species in the Middle East and Asia. They range in size from 2cm (¾in) to almost a metre (36in), and are found in virtually all types of tropical freshwater biotope and sometimes in brackish water. It is sometimes said that if there is a freshwater ecological niche, or a potential food item, a cichlid will have evolved to fill or eat it!

This has resulted in a quite astonishing diversity of form and habits, especially among lake-dwelling African species, but they nevertheless share one behavioural characteristic, which has endeared them to aquarists while causing the latter problems almost beyond imagination: they all guard their eggs and fry, often for weeks or even months – to the detriment of anything foolish enough to approach the brood, for example tankmates in captivity.

Cichlids are nevertheless one of the most popular groups, especially with aquarists who want something more challenging than a simple underwater scene. Some are also gorgeously coloured, and most show more interest in their owner than other fishes, giving them a decided air of intelligence. Large specimens can make excellent pets.

They have evolved two major breeding strategies, with many minor variations: **substrate-brooding**, where the eggs are laid on a plant, rock, or branch, and the resulting fry shepherded; and **mouthbrooding**, where eggs are taken into the mouth after spawning, and the fully developed, often independent fry are released three to five weeks later.

Pigeon blood discus
(Symphysodon aequifasciata *var.*)

Pearl cichlid (Geophagus brasiliensis)

SPECIAL CONSIDERATIONS IN CAPTIVITY

Although some species are relatively indestructible, many require not only correct water conditions but also a reasonable simulation of their natural surroundings in order to thrive.

However, far and away the most serious consideration must be the side-effects of their parental instincts. Even the smallest species commonly require 46cm (18in) or more of tank length to themselves when breeding, and are thus not suited to a small community aquarium. Some are highly territorial even when not breeding, and it can be difficult to persuade a male and female to accept each other. Many cichlids will reorganize their aquarium to provide a suitable nursery for their young, moving often prodigious quantities of substrate, undermining rockwork, uprooting plants, and, in the case of large individuals, even vandalizing equipment.

It is pointless to try and curb this strongly instinctive behaviour, but it can be managed, and most cichlid-keepers reckon the rewards outweigh the problems. Expert advice (from specialist books and experienced cichlid-keepers) is invaluable, even essential.

Breeding: Given the right environment and diet, and a compatible pair, breeding will usually occur. In the event of aggression by the male after spawning, he may have to be removed – in the case of substrate spawners – leaving the female to tend the eggs. In the case of mouthbrooders it is more usual to move the female to a separate brooding tank. Paternal and bi-parental mouthbrooders do not generally present this type of problem.

BRACKISH WATER FISHES

Orange chromide
(Etroplus maculatus)

Freshwater and marine fishes – with the exception of a few migratory species such as the eel (*Anguilla* spp.) and salmon (various *Salmo* spp.) – are generally restricted to one category or the other. The same cannot be said of brackish water fishes, which commonly live their lives in conditions of varying salinity, ranging from effectively nil to that of the sea. Some are representatives of otherwise freshwater families (e.g. Cichlidae); others have cousins in both fresh and salt water (e.g. puffers (Tetraodontidae). A few small families – **scats** (Scatophagidae), **monos** (Monodactylidae), **archerfishes** (Toxotidae), **mudskippers** (Periophthalmidae) – can be classed as truly brackish, although some of these (monos and scats) live in the sea as adults and usually only immatures are found in brackish or fresh water.

Their requirements are dealt with in detail in Chapter Eight (see page 118).

Giant gourami (Osphronemus goramy)

ANABANTIDS (LABYRINTH FISH)

This exclusively tropical group occurs only in Asia and Africa, and includes the gouramis (several families), paradise fish, combtails, and fighting fish (Belontidae), plus bush fish and climbing perch (Anabantidae). Some smaller species are excellent community fish, occupying the middle and upper layers of the aquarium.

Although diverse in size (2.5 to 70+cm; 1 to 30+in), appearance, and some habits, anabantids have the shared feature of being able to breathe atmospheric air, using a special organ called the labyrinth. This consists of a sac sited above the gills and containing additional gill-like structures designed to take up oxygen from air breathed in via the mouth. This permits survival in slow-moving or still, often stagnant habitats with oxygen-depleted water, such as irrigation ditches and rice paddies.

Many species feed mainly on insects, but others are herbivorous, omnivorous, or even predatory.

Care of eggs and fry is the norm, the male alone usually undertaking this role. In some species, a nest of bubbles is constructed, often among floating vegetation or debris, close to the surface where oxygen levels are highest. The eggs are placed, one by one, in this bubblenest by the male, and subsequently tended by him. Other species produce floating eggs which find their own way to the surface, where they are guarded by the male. Others are mouthbrooders.

SPECIAL CONSIDERATIONS IN CAPTIVITY

In many species atmospheric respiration is essential to survival, so an air space must be left between the surface and the cover glass. At the same time the tank should be kept covered so that the air breathed is at approximately tank temperature – chilling may damage the labyrinth and is lethal to fry.

Although many species originate from polluted waters and are also tolerant of a wide range of hardness and pH, some require specific water chemistry and/or excellent quality. In general the smaller species are the most delicate. And although paradise fish are noted for their tolerance of low temperatures, most anabantids are not so accommodating and require a minimum temperature of 24°C (75°F), often higher.

The long pelvic fins of gouramis, and the flowing finnage of the male Siamese fighting fish (*Betta splendens*) are often irresistible to other fishes; if nipping becomes a problem, it may be necessary to identify and remove the culprit(s).

Breeding: Bubblenest builders require suitable surface vegetation, and water movement should be minimal or eggs/fry may be swept away. Breeding males may become extremely hostile towards tankmates, and the female may not be tolerated once spawning is over; male fighting fishes will fight to the death even when not breeding, and should not be kept together.

Belontia hasselti

Paradise fish (Macropodus opercularis)

MARINE GROUPS

Unlike freshwater fishes, which derive from a huge variety of biotopes throughout the tropics, those marine fishes available to hobbyists through the aquarium trade derive almost exclusively from tropical coral reefs. In the aquarium literature they are normally (as here) grouped in individual families, whereas almost all of the freshwater groups contain several families.

SURGEONFISH
(ACANTHURIDAE)

So-called because they possess an extremely sharp, retractable, scalpel-like spine on either side of the caudal peduncle, these fish are very popular aquarium subjects, with common captive species measuring 10 to 25cm (4 to 10in).

Their slim, oval bodies are ideally suited to swimming in strong currents in search of their main food, algae. Being shoaling fish, they are often found in large numbers, sometimes with several species intermingling. Feeding takes place during the day with each individual using its special rasping teeth to scrape algae off the rocks. Surgeonfish have been likened to the cows of the sea, not only because they are mainly herbivorous but because they are constantly feeding. This is because algae, like grass, possesses very little nutritional value and a large quantity must be eaten to enable the fish to survive and grow.

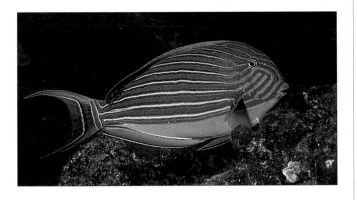

SPECIAL CONSIDERATIONS IN CAPTIVITY

Surgeonfish are prone to common diseases such as white spot and *Amyloodinium* (marine 'velvet', formerly *Oodinium*) if water quality is not maintained at a high level. To help avoid these ailments, the use of an ultraviolet sterilizer is recommended.

Adequate swimming space is required as well as a suitable diet. As we have already seen, algae is a favourite food but this is soon depleted in most aquaria. A good substitute is blanched lettuce or spinach.

Top left *Regal Tang* (Paracanthurus hepatus)
Top right *Pyjama Tang* (Acanthurus tennenti)
Above *Blue-banded surgeon* (Acanthurus lineatus)
Left *Purple surgeonfish* (Acanthurus xanthopterus)

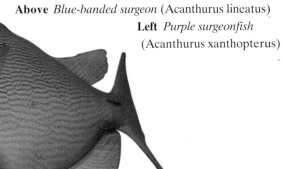

BLENNIES (BLENNIIDAE)

Blennies are a large family with over 300 recorded species in tropical and temperate waters. Many species found on or around the coral reef are very suitable for aquarium life, the average size of captive species being about 10cm (4in).

Most species have a poorly developed swim bladder and spend most of their time resting on the substrate or peering out of small crevices. Swimming is a laboured affair and is usually an ungainly hop from one location to another, although there are a few species which swim normally.

SPECIAL CONSIDERATIONS IN CAPTIVITY

Most blennies are ideal occupants for both the fish-only and invertebrate aquarium. Feeding is straightforward, with most species accepting frozen foods and marine flake.

Left Ecsenius bathi
Above *Yellow banded blenny* (Petroscirites breviceps)

BUTTERFLYFISH (CHAETODONTIDAE)

These lovely fish have long been favourites with marine aquarists owing to their exotic coloration and spectacular markings. Their bodies are always laterally compressed and many species have a medium to very long snout for probing cracks and crevices in search of small crustaceans, polyps and marine worms.

Strong pair bonds are often established in the wild and two fish can often be seen vigorously defending a territory from other similar species.

Sizes range from 10 to 20cm (4 to 10in) depending on species, and most can be kept in the aquarium, although the range of difficulty is vast, from straightforward to impossible! Fortunately, the most difficult butterflyfish have long since been identified and are rarely imported.

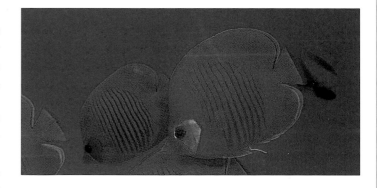

SPECIAL CONSIDERATIONS IN CAPTIVITY

All butterflyfish require excellent water quality, the best that the aquarist can provide. Even so, some species seem to survive well for a limited period and then die for no apparent reason.

It seems a shame that butterflyfish should be housed in the rather sterile fish-only aquarium, but corals and other invertebrates soon become the object of their feeding attention.

Only experienced and successful marine aquarists should consider keeping these beautiful fish.

Left Chaetodon *sp.*
Above *Lemonpeel butterflyfish* (Chaetodon semilarvatus)

TRIGGERFISH (BALISTIDAE)

Many fish in this family grow quite large (50cm+; 20in) and will prove to be well beyond the capabilities of the average hobbyist, but chosen with care, some smaller species (15 to 25cm; 6 to 10in), such as this Orangestriped triggerfish (**right**) are more manageable.

Whilst triggerfish have a justifiable reputation as the bullies of the marine aquarium, they should never be discounted as potential introductions to the fish-only set-up. Coloration and patterns can be nothing short of stunning in some species, in others a drab and dull appearance makes them somewhat less desirable.

The name triggerfish derives from the dorsal fin, which is generally carried flat in a groove in the body. When erected, however, it forms a trigger-like device that enables the fish to lock itself into a crevice, preventing its extraction by any predator.

Orange-striped triggerfish (Balistapus undulatus)

Additionally, any fish trying to swallow a triggerfish with its dorsal fin raised is usually deterred or at least distracted while the triggerfish makes good its escape.

Triggerfish have powerful teeth and jaws enabling them to feed on crustaceans, sea urchins and starfish.

SPECIAL CONSIDERATIONS IN CAPTIVITY

Triggerfish are aggressive towards members of their own family and should not be housed together or with other fish they might bully. Invertebrates are attacked and eaten, consequently a fish-only arrangement is the sole option.

Some species are very destructive towards aquarium 'furniture', and heaters, pipes and wiring may have to be protected from their attentions. Additionally, the aquarist may receive a nasty bite if the triggerfish are not treated with the required respect.

MANDARINFISH (CALLIONYMIDAE)

Mandarinfish are similar to some bottom-dwelling blennies but possess striking coloration and markings, an ideal camouflage for their life among beds of eelgrass. About 10cm (4in) in size, males and females are easily distinguished as the first dorsal ray on the male is greatly extended. Other fish tend to ignore mandarinfish because they possess an unpleasant-tasting mucus which can be shed in the face of any potential predator.

Above *Mandarinfish* (Synchiropus splendidus)

Below *Psychedelic fish* (Synchiropus picturatus)

SPECIAL CONSIDERATIONS IN CAPTIVITY

Difficulties in keeping mandarinfish successfully usually revolve around providing them with enough food. When housed in an established invertebrate aquarium, the fish can continuously browse on the many micro-organisms to be found there. Unfortunately, the fish-only aquarium is largely devoid of these organisms and the mandarinfish often slowly starve to death due to competition from tankmates.

Excellent water quality is essential at all times.

HAWKFISH (CIRRHITIDAE)

Owing to the lack of a fully developed swim bladder, hawkfish can swim only in short bursts, and spend most of their time perched on rocks or in the branches of gorgonians. From such vantage points they are able to spot potential prey and swoop down in much the same way as hawks. Shrimps and small fish are favourite foods, and are efficiently captured in extended jaws. Common captive species measure 7.5 to 10cm (3 to 4in).

SPECIAL CONSIDERATIONS IN CAPTIVITY

Hawkfish must not be housed in the same aquaria as shrimps or small fish since these are likely to prove irresistible as illicit meals. Gorgonians may also suffer if hawkfish continuously perch in their branches.

Left *Long-nosed hawkfish* (Oxycirrhites typus)
Below *Spotted hawkfish* (Cirrhitus splendens)

PORCUPINEFISH (DIODONTIDAE) AND PUFFERFISH (TETRAODONTIDAE)

Although these are different families, they are included under one heading owing to their similarities. They share the ability to inflate their bodies by gulping in water or air as a defensive strategy to avoid being eaten by predators. What appears a tasty mouthful becomes an unmanageable football and is soon released! In addition, porcupine-fish are armed with spines covering the whole body, while puffer-fish exude a toxic mucus from their skin. Both are designed to deter predators. The development of such devices is crucial as members of both families are sluggish swimmers and would otherwise become easy prey for any passing predator. Strong teeth and jaws are used to crack open the shells of crustaceans, and wherever possible, similar foods should be provided in the aquarium.

Common captive species measure 15 to 30cm (6 to 12in).

SPECIAL CONSIDERATIONS IN CAPTIVITY

Excellent water quality, plenty of swimming space, and peaceful tankmates are the keys to success.

As the teeth are constantly growing, it occasionally becomes necessary for a trained veterinarian to file them down. If this is not done, the fish cannot feed and slowly starves to death. Supplying molluscs and crustaceans in their shells can help to wear away these fishes' teeth.

Above *Porcupinefish* (Diodon liturosus)
Left *Masked pufferfish* (Arothron diadematus)

CARDINALFISH (APOGONIDAE)

These fish are perhaps one of the most straightforward to keep in the marine aquarium, although their colours are not always as vivid as other families and they have a tendency to remain stationary for long periods, making them rather inactive subjects. Those kept in the aquarium generally measure about 7.5cm (3in).

In the wild, many cardinalfish remain in the security of rocky overhangs or caves, sometimes in very large numbers. Often feeding at night, they rely on suitably sized planktonic animals being brought to them by the current.

Unusually for marine fish, cardinalfish are mouthbrooders, with male, female, or shared responsibility, depending on the species.

SPECIAL CONSIDERATIONS IN CAPTIVITY

Cardinalfish will not tolerate bullying so their compatibility with potential tankmates must be considered carefully.

Although largely nocturnal feeders in the wild, cardinalfish will successfully adapt to daytime feedings in the aquarium. Small pieces of meaty foods such as brine shrimp, mysis, and frozen plankton are eagerly accepted.

Left *Pyjama cardinalfish* (Sphaeramia nematoptera)

GOBIES (GOBIIDAE)

Lacking a swim bladder, gobies have little choice but to spend most of their lives close to or on the substrate. They are often to be seen swimming with brief, jerky movements as they travel from one place to another. Those kept in the aquarium usually fall into the 2.5 to 18cm (1 to 7in) size range.

Often confused with blennies, gobies can nearly always be distinguished by their two separate dorsal fins and their fused pelvic fins which form a sucker-like disc, a feature that enables them to cling to surfaces in the face of powerful water turbulence.

Some gobies live in a shared burrow with a shrimp. This fascinating relationship benefits both parties as the sharp-eyed goby stands guard, looking out for danger, while the short-sighted shrimp excavates and repairs the burrow.

SPECIAL CONSIDERATIONS IN CAPTIVITY

Most gobies will appreciate good water quality and peaceful tankmates.

As many species sift the sand through their gills for morsels of food, it would be unfair to keep these individuals in a tank without a sandy substrate.

Smaller species which grow no larger than 2.5cm (1in) are best kept in the absence of predatory fish or anemones, to which they may lose their lives.

Above *Lemon Goby* (Gobiodon citrinus)

Above *Blue-cheeked gobies* (Valenciennea strigata)

GRAMMAS (GRAMMIDAE) AND PYGMY BASSLETS (PSEUDOCHROMIDAE)

Again two families of fish have been combined for their common traits. Grammas are found only in the Caribbean, while pygmy basslets inhabit the Indo-Pacific and Red Sea regions. All are relatively small (5 to 13cm; 2 to 5in) and shy, patrolling the maze of connecting crevices within the reef in search of small crustaceans, marine worms and planktonic creatures.

Above *Royal Gramma* (Gramma loreto)

Many species are highly colourful but extremely territorial. They will often attack unrelated tankmates should they trespass.

SPECIAL CONSIDERATIONS IN CAPTIVITY
Unless the aquarium is especially large, it is recommended that only one species be kept if fighting is to be avoided.

Do not keep these species together with other families of fish having a similar shape or coloration e.g. some dwarf wrasse.

Above *Strawberry Gramma* (Pseudochromis porphyreus)

WRASSE (LABRIDAE)

There are over 400 species of wrasse known to science and the size range is enormous: 6cm to 2.1m (2.5in to 7ft)! Fortunately, there are a wide number of species suitable for aquarium life.

Wrasse are opportunist feeders with a broad appetite. Some act as cleaner fish, ridding other species of parasites, while others wander in search of just about anything edible.

Dwarf wrasse grow no bigger than 10cm (4in) and are highly desirable for the marine aquarium. Larger wrasse are often seen for sale as colourful tiny juveniles but they soon outgrow their allotted tank space and require re-housing.

Above *Blue spotted wrasse* (Anampses caeruleopunctatus)

SPECIAL CONSIDERATIONS IN CAPTIVITY
As night approaches, many wrasse protect themselves by hiding in the sand. These species need to be identified and a suitable sandy substrate provided.

Left *Pyjama Wrasse* (Pseudocheilinus hexataenia)

FIREFISH (MICRODESMIDAE)

Firefish are small (about 7.5cm/3in, for most captive species), elongated fish with an extended first dorsal ray which they flick up and down, possibly as a means of communication.

Large shoals hang in the current close to reef walls into which they can bolt should danger threaten. Never straying far from cover, firefish feed on planktonic animals brought to them by the current.

SPECIAL CONSIDERATIONS IN CAPTIVITY

Firefish require excellent water quality and sufficient crevices in which to hide. Some individuals may jump out of the aquarium, so cover glasses are recommended.

Right *Firefish* (Nemateleotris magnifica)

MORAY EELS (MURAENIDAE)

Moray eels are generally sedentary and occupy a favoured cave or crevice for long periods. Their colours and patterns are appealing to the hobbyist but even the smallest species achieves 30cm (12in), and most have the potential to exceed 90cm (36in).

They hunt for their prey of fish, crustaceans and molluscs by day or at night, depending on how hungry they are. Being extremely short-sighted, they rely on a keen sense of smell and constantly gape and lunge forward to 'taste the scent' of nearby objects. This may appear to be threatening behaviour but it is only a threat if you are something edible!

SPECIAL CONSIDERATIONS IN CAPTIVITY

The hobbyist who keeps a moray eel should remember several important points:

1) It can outgrow a small aquarium very quickly
2) It can bite (albeit unintentionally)
3) An uncovered aquarium is an invitation to slither out onto the carpet
4) A large appetite produces a great deal of waste and an efficient filtration system is required to dispose of it
5) Tankmates small enough to be eaten will be!

Left and above *Moray eels* (Gymnothorax *sp.*)

JAWFISH (OPISTOGNATHIDAE)

Jawfish are so called because they have large mouths in which to brood their eggs, not because they have particularly large appetites. In fact, they occupy burrows in the sand and feed on small planktonic particles drifting in the current. Common captive species measure about 12.5cm (5in).

SPECIAL CONSIDERATIONS IN CAPTIVITY

If a deep, sandy substrate cannot be provided for jawfish, in which to dig burrows, this species must be discounted as they are unlikely to survive for very long without burrows.

Jawfish may jump out of the aquarium, so close-fitting covers are essential.

Left *Yellow-headed jawfish* (Opistognathus aurifrons)

BOXFISH (OSTRACIIDAE)

Most of what has already been written about porcupinefish and pufferfish also applies to boxfish. One of the major differences is that boxfish cannot inflate, but instead possess hard skeletal plates just below the surface of the skin, which predators find difficult to crush. Combine this with a toxic mucus and you have a slow-swimming fish that most predators choose to avoid. Species kept in the aquarium average 10 to 40cm (4 to 16in).

Left *Spotted boxfish* (Ostracion *sp.*)
Above *Juvenile Yellow boxfish* (Ostracion cubicus)

SPECIAL CONSIDERATIONS IN CAPTIVITY

A fish-only tank is essential as boxfish will try to eat any corals or other invertebrates. Peaceful tankmates are also important as excessive bullying will cause the boxfish to shed its toxic mucus, killing itself and all of its companions!

ANGELFISH (POMACANTHIDAE)

This family of fishes contains some of the most popular marine species, and some of the most interesting. Split into two groups – the larger angelfish and the dwarf angelfish (those not exceeding 12.5cm; 5in) – there is a species for almost every eventuality.

The juveniles of many larger angelfish species have a different coloration to the adults – frequently white lines on a dark blue background, or yellow lines on black. It is thought that this difference allows them to mix freely with adults without being regarded as a threat and consequently being driven away.

The dwarf angelfish are nearly all members of the genus *Centropyge* and do not have a juvenile livery. They browse on small crustaceans, marine worms and algae in amongst the reef crevices. Larger angelfish are bold fish, swimming openly across

the reef, normally in mated pairs. Some species may attain 60cm (24in) when fully grown.

SPECIAL CONSIDERATIONS IN CAPTIVITY

Dwarf angelfish are ideally suited to the invertebrate aquarium as they will do no harm. The same cannot be said of the larger species which will eat most invertebrates. A fish-only aquarium is the safest place to accommodate them.

Many angelfish refuse to share a tank with the same, or similar, species. Care must be taken to ensure that compatible species or individuals are housed in the same tank.

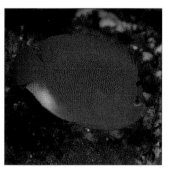

Above left *Juvenile Emperor angelfish* (Pomacanthus imperator)
Above right *Emperor angelfish* (Pomacanthus imperator)
Far left *Three-spot angelfish* (Apolemichthys trimaculatus)
Left *Regal angelfish* (Pygoplites diacanthus)

ANEMONEFISH AND DAMSELFISH (POMACENTRIDAE)

Without doubt, this family contains some of the most popular fish among marine hobbyists. The gaudy colours and markings of both anemonefish and damselfish have assured their high popularity.

The largest specimens rarely reach 10cm (4in) and can be accommodated easily.

In the wild, anemonefish, also known as clownfish, are always found in association with an anemone, as are some damselfish.

SPECIAL CONSIDERATIONS IN CAPTIVITY

Many damselfish are highly territorial and can bully other tankmates relentlessly. Such stress-inducing behaviour can cause disease and sometimes death in sensitive species.

Anemonefish are not quite so aggressive and they often fare better in an anemone. It must be noted that anemones are very sensitive invertebrates and require optimum water conditions for

good health. Merely adding one to a mainly fish-populated tank usually results in its early demise.

Left *Anemonefish* (Amphiprion ocellaris)
Above *Damselfish* (Pomacentridae) *in fright coloration.*

LIONFISH (SCORPAENIDAE)
(ALSO KNOWN AS DRAGONFISH OR SCORPIONFISH)

Lionfish are very decorative fish with greatly extended fin rays and striped markings. Such attractive features may belie the fact that they are highly efficient predators. Other fish and crustaceans form the main part of their diet and are efficiently captured in the capacious mouth. Their size ranges from 10 to 35cm (4 to 14in).

Being slow-swimming fish they may appear to be easy targets for larger predators. However, all members of the family Scorpaenidae possess venomous spines which provide adequate protection from all but the most determined enemy.

Lionfish (Pterois volitans)

SPECIAL CONSIDERATIONS IN CAPTIVITY

Newly imported specimens will often refuse to accept anything but live foods such as river shrimp and young fry. For the sake of convenience, the aquarist must 'convert' them to dead foods such as lancefish and mussels as soon as possible.

Safety has to be the main consideration when keeping lionfish. Spreading fin rays tipped with venom mean that hands must be kept well clear of these fish during in-tank maintenance.

Lionfish should never have tankmates which are small enough to be swallowed by them – because they will be swallowed!

SEA BASS AND GROUPERS (PLESIOPIDAE/SERRANIDAE)

These related families encompass a great number of species, many totally unsuited to aquarium life, although a few have proved to be very popular.

SPECIAL CONSIDERATIONS IN CAPTIVITY

Concerns regarding sea bass and groupers usually revolve around their eventual size. It is not unusual for them to grow to 30cm (12in), and some species are known to exceed 45cm (18in). In addition, most species are highly predatory and will soon clear an aquarium of fish small enough to be eaten. They need rocky reefs and crevices in which to shelter.

White-lined grouper (Epinephelus *sp.*)

SEAHORSES AND PIPEFISH (SYNGNATHIDAE)

Everyone loves a seahorse! Their extraordinary appearance and inherent charm has made them familiar to all. However, they are sensitive creatures and not easy to keep in captivity.

In the wild, they are often found inhabiting seagrass beds in sheltered areas. It is the males that carry the eggs in an abdominal brood pouch, eventually giving birth to live young. Recent research has revealed even more complex behavioural features and may eventually affect our desire to keep these beautiful fish in captivity.

Pipefish can be regarded as straightened-out seahorses. In fact, they are the evolutionary forerunners of the seahorses and their behaviour patterns are very similar.

Size range for those species commonly kept is 5 to 25cm (2 to 10in).

SPECIAL CONSIDERATIONS IN CAPTIVITY

As we have already seen, both seahorses and pipefish are extremely difficult to maintain in captivity. They require optimum water conditions, sufficient cover and the correct diet. Even so, a lifespan of about two years is all that can be expected.

Seahorse (Hippocampus *sp.*) *and Pipefish* (Syngnathus *sp.*)

DANGEROUS FISH

Every aquarist should be aware of the dangers associated with some fishes available for the aquarium. The carnivorous members of the piranha family are unpredictable, and may suddenly turn on tankmates or their owner's hand. Marine surgeonfish can lacerate their owner with their 'scalpels'. The electric catfish (*Malapterurus electricus*) and the electric eel (*Electrophorus electricus*) can deliver a powerful, possibly lethal, electric shock. The spines of some catfish can inflict a nasty puncture wound, sometimes injecting toxins; the same is true – only more so – of a number of marine fishes and invertebrates, some of which are potentially lethal. In the event that such a wound is received, soak it immediately in the hottest water bearable and seek immediate medical attention, giving details (its scientific name) of the species involved.

Obviously the greatest care should be taken when keeping such fishes, and it is essential to ensure that pets, children and unwary visitors cannot accidentally gain access to the aquarium.

In fact, many people would argue that such fishes should not be kept at all in a home with children.

Above right *Electric catfish* (Malapterurus electricus)
Right *Electric eel* (Electrophorus electricus)

CHAPTER EIGHT

A SELECTION OF BIOTOPE AQUARIA

As the years go by, if your interest in aquarium fish continues, you will find that you gradually assimilate all kinds of knowledge about them and their natural habitats. You may not, however, want to wait that long before attempting your first biotope aquarium; and the precise information you need may not be that easy to come by at this stage. You are likely to find either too little or so much that you cannot extract the vital essentials. So in this final chapter we will guide you through the basics of a number of different set-ups: rainforest, rocky lake shore, rapids, mangrove swamp, and, for marinists, several coral reef variants.

There are numerous other biotopes, but the above are the ones usually simulated. This may have something to do with their providing an attractive and interesting underwater scene, whereas an irrigation ditch, rice paddy, stagnant pool or muddy delta has fewer charms. We keep fish from all these biotopes, but we generally house them in compromise conditions, to which they normally adjust very well, having evolved a natural hardiness in order to survive in the often less than optimum conditions in their original homes.

Imitation tufa rock

Always remember that our chosen biotopes are 'blanket' headings: for example, the rainforest of the Amazon basin may be different in many respects from that of West Africa, and both will contain a number of habitats. For this reason we will, in each case, briefly define the habitat we are attempting to simulate, to avoid any confusion.

You can, of course, go one step further and set up a specific rather than a general biotope aquarium, i.e. one which contains only fish – and plants – found together in a single habitat in a single geographical locality (sympatric). There are, however, advantages to the generalized biotope – your choice of flora and fauna will not be so limited (and availability can be a

The fresh water of a river mingles with the salty water of the sea, resulting in a transition zone of brackish water.

real problem), and it may be easier to achieve fish compatibility. Sympatric species which compete for territory in the wild will probably do likewise in the aquarium, but won't automatically recognize a 'rival' from elsewhere as such.

We will provide a list of fish suited to each biotope; these lists are not, however, exhaustive catalogues, and, more important, they do not imply compatibility except in biotope requirements. The actual selection of fish must be researched by the aquarist.

Much of the information you will need to create your biotope aquarium has already been provided earlier in this book, hence although we will tell you what water parameters you will require, we will leave you to reread Chapter One to find out how to provide them. Likewise much of the equipment required will be standard to any aquarium, so we will mention only special requirements for each biotope. And we will not explain every stage of setting up, but simply draw your attention to points where this may differ from 'normal'.

You are, of course, at liberty to design your own layout based on the basic ideas and principles outlined here. Indeed, we hope you will do so, as that is a major part of the fun and interest of fishkeeping – and in Nature too, every little piece of biotope is different from the next.

Hygrophila *sp., a popular freshwater aquarium plant.*

BIOTOPE 1 - RAINFOREST

Habitat simulated: The bank zone of a small, slow-moving stretch of 'blackwater' (= soft, acid, stained brown by organic matter) river in the rainforest, at the point where it enters a small clearing.

Natural examples: Much of the Amazon basin; parts of the lowland coastal strip of West Africa between Liberia and the River Congo; parts of Madagascar and Indonesia.

Important features: Soft, slightly to very acid, slow-moving water; low light intensity where banks are tree-lined, with cover provided by tangles of roots, dead branches and trailing terrestrial vegetation (live trees); marginal and aquatic plants where more light penetrates. The bottom is fine gravel or sand, covered in part with a layer of leaf litter.

TYPICAL FISH

Characins: tetras, pencilfish, hatchetfish, piranhas.

Catfish: *Farlowella* (twig catfish), *Sturisoma, Rinelocaria, Ancistrus* (bristle-nose cats), *Dysichthys* (banjo cats), and some *Synodontis* (e.g. *Synodontis angelicus, Synodontis nigriventris*), are particularly suitable, but most soft, acid water species will be at home in this aquarium.

Cichlids: Discus (*Symphysodon* spp.) angels (*Pterophyllum* spp.), and both South American and West African dwarfs (e.g. *Apistogramma, Laetacara* (dwarf acaras), *Cleithracara* (keyholes), *Pelvicachromis, Thysochromis* and *Anomalochromis*). Some (but not all) larger species from this type of biotope, e.g. *Astronotus* (oscars) and *Uaru*, may demolish plants, which should therefore be omitted.

Cyprinodonts: Although this is not necessarily their natural habitat, many acid water killifish (*Aphyosemion, Rivulus,*

A female Pelvicachromis taeniatus

Harlequin rasboras (Rasbora heteromorpha)

Nothobranchius) will enjoy such an aquarium, which can be used to house these fishes when they are not busy in their breeding tanks.

Other groups: Representatives of other fish families may also be present, though generally in smaller numbers than those named above.

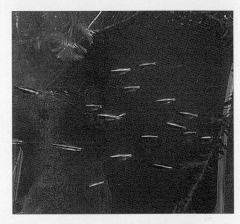
Neon tetras (Paracheirodon innesi)

Angelfish varieties (Pterophyllum scalare *var.*)

Borelli's dwarf cichlid (Apistogramma borellii)

FRESHWATER BIOTOPES

DESIGNING THE SIMULATION

One or two problem areas should be immediately apparent – decomposing tree leaves and trailing terrestrial vegetation would be potential sources of toxicity in a small volume of water. Instead we normally use as dark a substrate material as possible, while floating plants, Java fern (*Microsorium pteropus*), which can be grown on bogwood, and long-stemmed plants with floating leaves (e.g. dwarf waterlilies and *Nymphaea* species), provide necessary greenery in the upper layers.

Our design represents the edge of a small clearing on the river bank, and so includes both a dimly lit tree-shaded area and a more open space with vegetation. A 'root tangle' of bogwood is a major feature.

Variations: If the aquarium is to accommodate larger species, the décor must permit plenty of swimming space, and the root tangle may have to become a 'fallen branch', i.e. a large piece of wood with space in front and behind.

Water parameters: 0–5 dH, pH 5.5–6.8
Temperature: 24 –27°C (76–82°F).

DÉCOR

Substrate: Dark, hardness-free, fairly fine gravel or sand.

Background: This should be dark and 'earthy': the outside rear glass can be painted black or dark brown; dark brown carpet or cork tiles stained dark brown can be glued to the outside; or strips of cork bark can be glued, with spots of silicone sealant, to the inside. Ideally the end glass at the 'root tangle' end will also be covered.

Main décor: Bogwood and cork bark – it is worth shopping around and, if necessary paying extra, for a really good, large, root-like piece of bogwood, as well as a few smaller pieces. Plants as mentioned above, plus an additional selection of plants of varying heights for the more brightly lit area.

Black gravel

Sand

Bogwood

1

2

1. Mix black gravel and river sand to create a dappled light effect.

2. Plant after having created a 'natural tangle' of bogwood.

EQUIPMENT

Our design is for a 120cm (48in) aquarium, but the principles can be adapted to any size.

Filtration: The filter should be low-turnover and provide acidification via peat: air-driven UG supplemented by peat-filled box filters, or an external canister filter.

Lighting: One 105cm (42in) and one 60cm (24in) fluorescent.

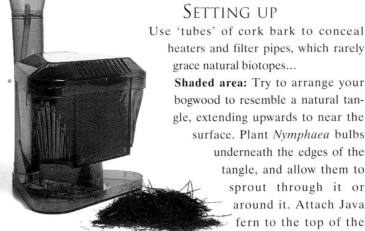

Internal canister filter with peat.

SETTING UP

Use 'tubes' of cork bark to conceal heaters and filter pipes, which rarely grace natural biotopes...

Shaded area: Try to arrange your bogwood to resemble a natural tangle, extending upwards to near the surface. Plant *Nymphaea* bulbs underneath the edges of the tangle, and allow them to sprout through it or around it. Attach Java fern to the top of the bogwood, using cotton or nylon fishing line to hold the plants in place. Once they have rooted, the cotton/nylon can be snipped away. If an internal cork bark background has been used, wedge Java fern into cracks – it will grow there happily.

Clearing: There would still be roots along the bank in a clearing, so include an extra piece of bogwood towards the rear of the planted area.

Lighting: Arrange the fluorescents so that the open area is lit by two, to aid plant growth, while only the longer tube extends over the root tangle.

Vallisneria

Water weed
(Elodea densa)

Acorus variegata *is a marsh plant which can be used in aquaria, but will need to be replaced annually.*

Java Fern Microsorium pteropus

Hemigraphis colorata *(broadleaf)*

MAINTENANCE

This type of aquarium is normally easy to maintain, the main consideration being the maintenance of the correct water chemistry. Peat becomes exhausted after a few weeks, and needs to be replaced – it is advisable to check pH regularly in order to know when to do so. Occasionally the pH in an acid water aquarium fluctuates violently or becomes too low, in which case a small bag of coral sand or other calciferous material can be suspended in the tank or placed in the filter to act as a pH buffer.

It may be necessary to fertilize the plants, and to prune/thin them to retain the original effect and avoid the aquarium becoming choked with jungle. In nature they would be 'pruned' by passing herbivores.

3

4

3. *Add matured water on a plate so as not to disturb the substrate.*

4. *Release the fish into the matured tank.*

A RAINFOREST BIOTOPE TANK

BIOTOPE 2 - ROCKY LAKE SHORE

Habitat simulated: A section of rocky shore in a large lake of the 'inland sea' type. The rather precipitous rocky shoreline continues down beneath the surface, and is washed by sometimes violent waves. Jumbles of fallen rocks on the sandy bottom, and holes in the underwater rock wall, provide shelter for numerous small cichlids.

Natural examples: Parts of the shoreline of the East African Rift Valley lakes (e.g. lakes Malawi, Tanganyika and Victoria).

Important features: Rockwork on a grand scale, with numerous cracks and crannies; hard alkaline water with a very high oxygen content – large lakes have tides and may be storm-tossed, with surf where waves break against rocky shoreline.

TYPICAL FISH

These lakes are dominated by **cichlids**, some of which have become very popular aquarium fish, many quite unsuitable for a general community so that this particular biotope aquarium is common in the hobby. It is important to realize that not all the cichlids available from these lakes are from this biotope, and that those from different biotopes are commonly incompatible with rock dwellers in terms of behaviour as well as habitat – in particular, rock-dwelling mouthbrooders are notoriously aggressive.

Lake Malawi: Cichlids of the rock-dwelling mbuna group, e.g. *Pseudotropheus, Melanochromis, Labeotropheus, Labidochromis, Iodotropheus, Cynotilapia, Petrotilapia.*

Lake Tanganyika: Rock-dwelling cichlids of the genera *Tropheus, Petrochromis, Neolamprologus, Lamprologus, Julidochromis, Telmatochromis, Chalinochromis, Cyprichromis* and *Paracyprichromis.*

Note: Not all members of all these genera are rockdwellers.

Lake Victoria: Rock-dwelling mouthbrooding cichlids of the genus *Haplochromis.*

Other fish: The cuckoo catfish, *Synodontis multipunctatus* (Lake Tanganyika) is commonly and successfully kept, with cichlids, in this type of aquarium.

Avoid mixing cichlids from different lakes.

Left *The Malawi 'red zebra'* Pseudotropheus (Maylandia) estherae

Below Julidochromis regani, *a Lake Tanganyika rock cichlid.*

Melanochromis auratus *(female) above,* Pseudotropheus lombardoi *(male) below*

Neolamprologus tretocephalus, *from Lake Tanganyika.*

Labidochromis caeruleus *is one of the most popular rock-dwelling Malawi cichlids.*

DESIGNING THE SIMULATION

It is essential to think big for this aquarium, which will be dominated by rockwork to the exclusion of all else. The size of the 'caves' (holes between the rocks), however, should be matched to the size of the proposed occupants. Some small Tanganyikan species prefer very small cracks.

Although such an underwater rockery may look stark and bare initially, after a few months algae will have started to coat the stone, giving it a mellower look. Algae should be welcomed – many rocky habitat species like to nibble it.

The lighting will be subdued – under bright light many of these fishes look 'washed out' and lose a lot of their brilliant metallic iridescence, which is intended to make them conspicuous in deeper, darker areas of the natural habitat.

Variations: Tanganyika substrate-spawners can be given two to three smaller rockpiles instead of one large edifice, so that a good area of substrate is left open for a pair or colony of shell-dwellers. Escargot shells are ideal for these.

Water parameters: Variably hard and alkaline.
Lake Malawi: 7–10 dGH, pH 7.8–8.5;
Lake Tanganyika: 15–20 dGH, pH 7.8–9.0;
Lake Victoria: 6–9 dGH, pH 7.1–7.8.
In practice hardness is not critical, but pH *must* remain alkaline. The water should be highly oxygenated and of extremely high quality.
Temperature: 26–27°C (78–82°F).

DÉCOR

Substrate: Gravel or sand; colour unimportant. Ten to 25% calciferous material (coral sand, crushed shell, limestone chips) may be incorporated in the substrate as a pH buffer. *Do not* use coral gravel (it is sharp, cuts digging mouths, lodges in gullet), and avoid substrates entirely of coral sand – as well as being glaringly white, its tiny particles can become suspended in the water and cause gill irritation (and damage), symptomized by constant scratching.
Background: This can be a plain dark background (e.g. external black or dark grey paint), or can continue the rock theme. Use an external printed 'rocky' background,

Imitation tufa rock

Smooth river rocks

1. Lay down the undergravel filter plates.

2. Smooth out the substrate.

3. Build up the rockwork, ensuring it is stable.

1

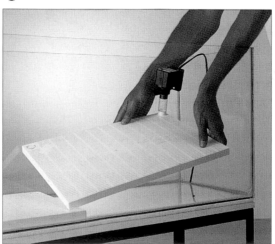

2

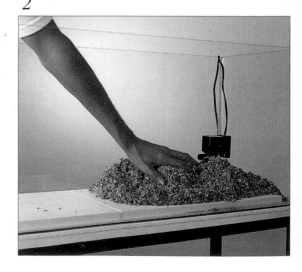

or line the inside of the back and end glasses with pieces of slate, which will also serve to protect the glass against leaning (or toppling) rockwork. Alternatively, sculpt styrofoam or mould fibreglass to simulate a rockface, remembering that any colourings and finishes (e.g. varnish) used must be nontoxic.

Main décor: Tufa rock, a kind of porous, and thus lightweight, limestone is commonly used, but does not provide the smooth spawning surfaces required by Tanganyika substrate-spawners, whose rockwork should, therefore, include at least some smooth surfaces, e.g. pieces of slate or flowerpots concealed among the tufa. Other types of rock can be used. Try to include plenty of large pieces, for effect and structural stability. Plants are totally out of place in this biotope simulation.

Shell grit mixture

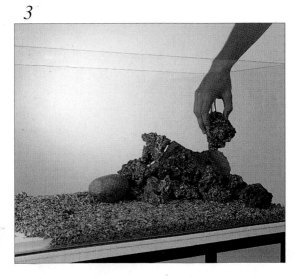

Lava rock

3

· EQUIPMENT

Our design is based on a 120 x 45 x 45cm (48 x 18 x 18in) aquarium; for mouthbrooders tank length should be at least 90cm (36in), better 120cm (48in).

Filtration: A powerful external filter with spray bar return, or UG filtration with twin powerheads. The canister filter may contain calciferous material (see under 'substrate', above) as a pH buffer.

Lighting: A single 90cm (36in) fluorescent.

Heating: Undertank heater mats are an advantage, avoiding the need to find space for immersion heaters among the copious rockwork. Alternatively it is possible to buy large external canister filters with integral heaters.

Other: If using an external filter, choose UG plates or other nontoxic plastic (e.g. thin styrofoam) to protect the tank bottom from sharp rocks.

SETTING UP

Position UG plates or protective plastic to cover the entire bottom to protect against rock points – remember not just the weight of that rock, but of the entire structure, will be bearing down on your base rocks. Add about 1cm (½in) of substrate and position any internal background and your 'foundation rocks', which should be large pieces with a flattish side facing downwards. Work them down into the substrate, then add the remainder of the latter.

Next, build your rockwork upwards, ensuring that each piece fits snugly and securely onto those supporting it – trial and error will be necessary. If using tufa rock this can be leaned against the back and ends of the aquarium; but this is inadvisable with denser, heavier rocks, in which case the structure should be free-standing, although some pieces may contact an internal background, particularly at the ends, as you want the effect of a rock wall running from end to end rather than a central pile. UG uplift tubes and heater/stats can be positioned behind pieces of slate placed diagonally across rear corners; the slate adds to the 'rock wall' effect so it isn't obvious that there is an empty space behind.

Rocks can be siliconed together, but this will make it extremely difficult to 'break down' the tank when required, and impossible to remove a single rock or two to catch fish. Avoid creating 'see-through' caves and arches; cichlids prefer dark culs-de-sac, where they cannot be attacked from behind and have just one entrance to defend.

FRESHWATER BIOTOPES

A ROCKY LAKE SHORE BIOTOPE TANK

BIOTOPE 3 - RAPIDS

Habitat simulated: An area of very fast-flowing river where it descends steeply, often through a gorge, sometimes with waterfalls. The riverbed, a mixture of rock and sand, is invariably littered with boulders, and water-worn outcrops from the rocky banks protrude into the edges of the stream. These rocky obstructions add to the turbulence of the main current, although there may be sheltered 'backwaters' in the lee of large outcrops.

Natural examples: There can be few rivers that do not have an area of rapids in their courses, even if only in miniature where their headwaters run rapidly downstream over pebbles. Notable areas of rapids, home to fish available in the aquarium trade, are found in the Congo and Volta basins in Africa, and in some of the tributaries of the Amazon in South America.

Important features: Water-worn rocks, currents and high oxygen levels. Algae are common, but higher plants are rare except in calm marginal pockets.

TYPICAL FISH

A number of fish families have evolved rheophilic (= current-loving) species, commonly with physical and behavioural adaptations to their unusual habitat, but at present their aquarium representatives are limited chiefly to cichlids. Fish are imported because of known demand, and cichlids are generally a very popular family with specialist aquarists.

The **cichlids** include *Steatocranus*, *Teleogramma*, fluviatile *Lamprologus*, and *Orthochromis* from Africa; *Teleocichla*, *Retroculus*, and some *Crenicichla* species from South America.

As rheophilic aquaria increase in popularity it is likely that other rheophiles will be imported as well.

These include some **catfishes** (including *Chrysichthys* and some *Synodontis*, *Chiloglanis*, *Euchilichthys* and *Doumea*), some **elephantnoses** (*mormyrids*), some 'sharks' (genus *Labeo*), and some **spiny eels** (*Mastacembelus*).

Many stretches of rapids are relatively, or totally, unexplored ichthyologically (especially in South America), so there may be many interesting fishes to come.

A female Steatocranus irvinei *guards her fry beneath a water-worn boulder.*

A female Orthochromis machadoi *brooding eggs.*

Nanochromis nudiceps *are found in calm pools at the edge of rapids.*

A male Steatocranus ubanguiensis.

A female Teleogramma brichardi *in breeding colour.*

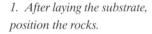

1. After laying the substrate, position the rocks.

2. Wedge bogwood between the rocks.

3. Add water by pouring onto the rock so as not to disturb the substrate.

4. Release fishes into mature water when the tank has settled.

DESIGNING THE SIMULATION

Obviously there are limits to the degree of current and turbulence that can be created in a small glass box, but this is not a serious problem, as rheophilic species do not actually live in the main current – they would be swept away! They are instead found in the lee of or under rocks, or in the relatively calm layer between the torrent and its bed, and sometimes have special modifications (e.g. shape, suckers, lack of buoyancy) to enable them to remain in these areas.

As with the previous biotope, the emphasis here is again on rocks, but as this will be an aquarium with a lower fish population it will not be necessary to create a rock wall with numerous interstices. Instead create a jumble of water-worn boulders, here and there rising towards the surface (= the top of the 'safe' water layer, in nature), as some rheophiles are noted for their apparent enjoyment of 'perching' in elevated spots.

A piece of bogwood may be added to simulate a tree branch that has been swept downstream and wedged among the rocks. Plants are inappropriate, but algal growth on the rocks can be encouraged.

Lighting should be moderate, as the only shade will be under rocks, and we want to encourage the fish to perch in the open as well.

Water parameters: Obviously rapids will share the water chemistry of the river in which they are situated, which is thus variable. Most of the rheophilic species currently available are known to come from soft, neutral or slightly to very acid water (although some of the African species have been found to live and breed happily in hard alkaline conditions): hence hardness 0–6 dGH, and pH 6.0–7.0. The water should be very highly oxygenated and have a current, but not violent turbulence.
Temperature: 24 –27°C (75–82°F).

DÉCOR

Substrate: Hardness-free sand or fine gravel. Avoid sharp edges as some rheophilic species burrow head-first under rocks. The colour of this base substrate is immaterial, as it will be largely concealed by boulders, and pebbles in open areas.
Background: As for the rocky lake shore aquarium.
Main décor: Non-calciferous rocks, preferably water-worn and rounded, of varying sizes, plus a good scattering of smaller pebbles of the same shape. This set-up is most effective if the boulders are all of the same rock and contrast with the substrate where this shows through the pebbles. Obtaining suitable rounded rocks will generally involve collecting them yourself, and a certain amount of geological knowledge is useful. It is not environmentally friendly to collect suitable stones from streams, where they are probably home to

1

2

indigenous fauna. However, the beach can provide excellent large and small pebbles. Wash them well to remove all traces of salt.

A piece of bogwood may also be included in this aquarium, preferably a long thin piece that can realistically simulate a dead branch jammed in between rocks.

EQUIPMENT

Rheophilic cichlids are often solitary except when breeding, and will squabble if space is too restricted. At the same time they require only very small territories, so six to eight individuals can be kept in a 120cm (48in) aquarium, although a male and female of the same species would probably fight continuously if 'crowded' into a 60cm (24in) tank. A good

Silica sand

Water-worn rocks

basic size for this biotope is 120 x 40 x 40cm (48 x 15 x 15in); extra width is preferable to extra depth for these rather 'two-dimensional' fish.

Filtration: UG powered by twin powerheads, or a large, high-turnover, external canister, with the water returned via a spray bar or spray bar and trickle filter tray.

Lighting: Use a single 90 or 105cm (36 or 42in) fluorescent.

SETTING UP

Because the main décor is smooth rounded rocks, and the volume of rockwork is smaller, it is not so important to protect the tank bottom as for the lake biotope. Put in a 1cm (½in) layer of substrate and any internal background. Then arrange large 'boulders' on the bottom, close together in places, working them down into the substrate.

Next add the remainder of the substrate. Place further large boulders on top of those bedded in the substrate, to create caves. The tops of these upper boulders will also provide 'perches'. Bed a few smaller rocks in the open substrate and scatter pebbles on any remaining open space.

Wedge the 'tree branch' in place – between a 'top rock' and the back of the tank is a good place, and it can be used to conceal internal equipment. Otherwise, conceal equipment in corners, as for Biotope Two (see page 109).

Large rocks are more effective

MAINTENANCE
No special maintenance points.

3

4

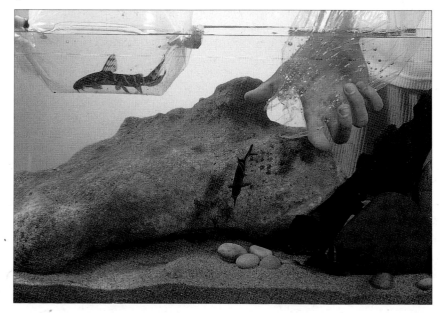

A RAPIDS BIOTOPE TANK

BIOTOPE 4 - MANGROVE SWAMP

Habitat simulated: A small area of tidal mangrove swamp where a slow-moving river flows into the sea.

Natural examples: Mangrove swamps are common in the tropics where slow-moving rivers enter the sea via deltas or other low-lying terrain. They are also found along sheltered sea shores, where there are no river estuaries.

Important features: At high tide the roots of the mangrove trees are partially submerged, but are exposed as the water level falls, as are areas of muddy substrate. Water chemistry also varies, as regards salinity, according to the level of the tide, with only residual salt at low water. This is essentially a wood, water and mud biotope, lacking aquatic plants because of the variable water chemistry. Above water the vegetation may be lush, with epiphytic plants (e.g. orchids, ferns).

The ecology of the fauna may reflect the constant variation in water level.

TYPICAL FISH

Archerfish (*Toxotes*), mudskippers (*Periophthalmus*), four-eyes (*Anableps*), monos (*Monodactylus*), and scats (*Scatophagus*).

Some (but not all) gobies (Gobiidae), puffers (Tetraodontidae) and shark catfish (*Arius*), plus cichlids of the genus *Etroplus* (actually from brackish lagoons and estuaries), can also be kept in this biotope.

Some rainbowfishes (Melanotaenidae) sometimes occur in slightly brackish conditions, but are usually kept in fresh water, with a little salt optional.

Mudskipper (Periophthalmus *sp.*)

Pink-tailed Australian rainbowfish (Melanotaenia splendida)

Fiddler crabs do not mix well with fish in an aquarium set-up and it is best to have them on their own.

Mono (Monodactylus argenteus)

Banded rainbow (Melanotaenia trifasciata)

Archerfish (Toxotes *sp.*) *firing a water jet*

BRACKISH WATER BIOTOPE

DESIGNING THE SIMULATION

Several major problems should be immediately apparent: although tidal conditions are sometimes simulated in large public and scientific aquaria, this is impracticable (though not impossible if you want a challenge) in the domestic set-up. The same applies to the accompanying variation in salinity, and it is normal to compromise (see 'water parameters', below). Mud is not generally included in aquaria because of the effect on water clarity.

Less obvious problems are that some species have evolved 'extra-aquatic' habits to suit their variable biotope: mudskippers live in extremely shallow water with their eyes protruding, and sometimes skip across open exposed mud, hence their name; four-eyes swim at the surface with the upper part of their eyes out of the water; and archerfish shoot down insects from above-water vegetation with a jet of water. These requirements must be satisfied, plus the exposed eyes (and bodies) of some of these creatures require warm humid air above the surface of the water.

The 'extra-aquatic' species require what is termed a paludarium (*palus* is the Latin word for swamp), a tank which is only part-filled with water, leaving a large airspace above the water's surface. Fine sand is used instead of mud, and the décor is structured so that species that wish to crawl out of the water can do so onto large flat stones or pieces of wood, or, with a little ingenuity, areas of sand. .

The decoration is primarily of bogwood, and should continue above the water's surface. Indeed, some paludaria have large pieces of bogwood or cork bark protruding above the top of the aquarium and planted with ferns and orchids, which enjoy the humidity. Great care should be taken with the use of terrestrial vegetation, however, because of the risk of poisoning (consult an expert tropical botanist or horticulturist if possible). And remember, mudskippers and four-eyes require a humid atmosphere, which means a cover unless the tank is situated in a humid room (tropical greenhouse). Nevertheless, cover glasses can be fitted discretely around such a wood/plant feature out of normal frontal viewing.

There is little point in keeping archerfish unless you provide them with insects to shoot down, and something on which those insects can perch. A *tight-fitting* cover is required to keep archerfish prey in the paludarium. The necessary vegetation can be plastic; marginal plants grown emerse in containers of compost and water/sprayed with fresh water; or epiphytic, with the same health warning as above.

This is one set-up where there is vast scope for ingenuity and personal design!

Water parameters: In Nature, the fish may be subject to almost marine salinity at high tide, but at low tide their water will be that of the river (i.e. it could be soft or hard, acid or alkaline), plus residual salt leaching from the mud. Most brackish aquaria use local tap water with a compromise salinity of 50% that of marine conditions (see page 128, Marine Biotopes), on the basis that while they have evolved to deal with habitat extremes, their 'norm' is a median figure. There should be minimal water movement.

Temperature: Should be a little higher than for many aquaria, 26–28°C (78–84°F).

DÉCOR

Substrate: Fine sand, mud-coloured if possible.

Background: As for the rainforest biotope.

Main décor: Bogwood and cork bark will predominate. If keeping mudskippers you will need at least one large flat surface, which can be a piece of slate, flattish piece of bogwood, artfully shaped piece of marine grade ply varnished with marine varnish (but without any (toxic) anti-fouling agent), or a (nontoxic) plastic tray of sand. Sand can be sprinkled on wet varnish or a thin layer of silicone sealant, to keep it in place.

Several mudskippers will require several platforms or a very large one, as they can be territorial.

Moss

Bogwood

Acorus variegata,
a marsh plant

Fine sand

Non-aquatic fern

Tangled branch

Slate

**BRACKISH WATER
BIOTOPE**

*A spray bar and pipe for use
with an external canister filter.*

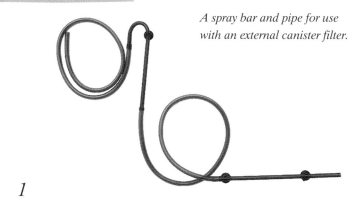

1

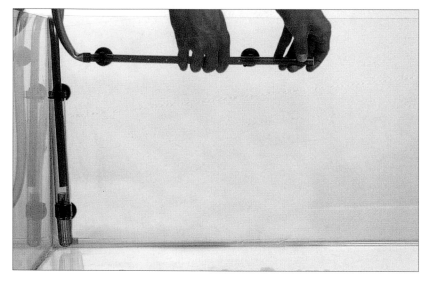

2

EQUIPMENT

The tank should be large and deep, in order to have sensible areas above and below the water's surface. If it is impossible to accommodate a deep aquarium, then only smaller, shallow-water or surface-dwelling species will be possible. Suggested size: 120 x 45 x 60cm (48 x 18 x 24in) deep, or 180 x 60 x 90cm (72 x 24 x 36in) for a real showpiece.

Filtration: This is probably best provided by a large-capacity but low-turnover external canister, with its return split so as to return part of the water below the surface, the remainder above via a spray bar or trickle tray. Aim to create a dripping effect as from damp vegetation. But if using real plants ensure that they are not sprayed with brackish water!

Lighting: An enclosed tank can be lit with fluorescents as usual, but it is better to use spotlights or suspended lamps to provide sufficient light intensity for the vegetation and to illuminate the very deep tank.

1. Attach the spray bar.

2. Bury rocks in the mud-coloured sandy substrate.

3. Form the raised section to resemble a mud flat.

4. Plant the grasses and ferns in troughs of compost above the water level, after positioning the bogwood and the branch in such a way as to conceal this.

3

SETTING UP

In the case of this biotope, procedure will depend to a considerable extent on your chosen design and décor. This aquarium is, as already stated, an opportunity for inventiveness. Simply remember always to follow the basic rules of fishkeeping: especially 'fish come first' and 'nothing toxic'.

Some of your décor may need to support the mudskipper platform(s), which should dip beneath the surface at one point and meld into the other décor, just as an area of mud would tail off into roots and vegetation. If you are intending to grow live plants in troughs at the rear, it might be helpful to silicone a glass shelf in place to carry these, just above your intended water level. Obviously none of your shelves and troughs should be visible when the set-up is complete.

Arrange your lighting so that plants receive adequate light but fish have a choice of 'sun' or shade.

MAINTENANCE

You may need periodically to clean away a 'tide-line' of salt from the front glass at water level. Regular daily plant care may be necessary (spraying or watering), with periodic pruning – or replacement of less rampant specimens, as some plants will not live forever in their emerse state. There are tremendous opportunities for aquatic horticulture here, allowing plants to follow their natural cycle with an emerse period in the paludarium and an aquatic phase in a conventional aquarium. To avoid root disturbance they must be grown in containers.

Feeding: Archers and mudskippers are insectivores. Crickets can be purchased for feeding reptiles, but you can experiment with woodlice, houseflies and other 'free produce'. Avoid any insect that uses poison to defend itself or stun prey, just in case this is toxic when ingested. If the tank isn't 'sealed' and extra-aquatic prey are therefore impracticable, then these fishes will also relish aquatic invertebrates and insect larvae.

4

BRACKISH WATER
BIOTOPE

A MANGROVE SWAMP BIOTOPE TANK

BIOTOPE 5 - THE TRUE CORAL REEF

NOTE

The following biotope examples begin with the most difficult and end with the most straightforward. The newcomer would do well to start with the latter.

Habitat simulated: The archetypal reef community. A rocky wall festooned with soft and hard corals, sponges, sea whips and sea fans. The rocks contain many caves and crevices which provide a home for shy colourful fishes, shrimps, crabs and numerous other creatures.

Natural examples: Found in the shallow seas all around the world between the tropics of Cancer and Capricorn. Coral reefs normally surround islands or atolls but they also form in shallow coastal waters where conditions are suitable. Well-known locations include the Great Barrier Reef, the Philippines, the Seychelles, the Caribbean islands, the Red Sea, the Maldives and Hawaii.

Important features: Coral reefs are remarkably stable biotopes – little changes from month to month, and there are no significant seasonal changes such as occur in temperate latitudes or in rivers or swamps. Sea temperatures are warm and generally stable throughout the year to within a few degrees. Sunlight penetrates the water with the same intensity and quality 365 days of the year (give or take the odd storm!). Most reef animals can be found inhabiting the areas from the low tide mark to only a few metres deeper. As we descend below this surface layer, the number of species diminishes steadily until the lack of sunlight results in a rather sterile environment by comparison.

Coral reefs are constructed largely by the animals that live on them. Coral polyps produce calcareous skeletons in which to live, and colonies of the same species form the characteristic different corals which astound us with their variety and beauty. When they die, new corals form on the old skeletons and so the reef is built up. Some reefs form on the encircling rocks of a submerged collapsed volcano rim. In fact, corals will inhabit any suitable structure if it is situated in the right place: oil platform legs, shipwrecks, piers and jetties, breakwaters, even old tyres or concrete blocks! The latter have been deliberately dumped in parts of the Caribbean and Gulf of Mexico to replace reefs that have been destroyed by industrial pollution and hurricanes, or to create new reefs.

TYPICAL FISH

Surgeonfish (Acanthuridae), cardinalfish (Apogonidae), triggerfish (Balistidae), blennies (Blenniidae), butterflyfish (Chaetodontidae), hawkfish (Cirrhitidae), grammas (Grammidae), squirrelfish (Holocentridae), wrasse (Labridae), firefish (Microdesmidae), moray eels (Muraenidae), angelfish (Pomacanthidae), anemonefish and damselfish (Pomacentridae), basslets (Pseudochromidae), lionfish/dragonfish (Scorpaenidae) and sea bass (Serranidae).

Powder-blue surgeonfish
(Acanthurus leucosternon)

Red starfish
(Fromia elegans)

Long-nosed butterflyfish
(Forcipiger flavissimus)

Orange-lined cardinalfish
(Archamia fucata)

Sea squirt
(Polycarpa *sp.*)

Sabre-toothed squirrelfish (Holocentridae)

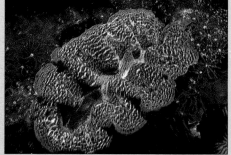

Blue/gold clam (Tridacna sp.)

Cleaner shrimp (Lysmata amboinensis)

TYPICAL INVERTEBRATES

Sponges (Porifera); hard corals (Scleractina); gorgonians (Gorgonidae); mushroom corals (Actinodiscidae); anemones (Actinaria); star polyps (Clavulariidae); pulse corals (Xeniidae); soft corals (*Sarcophyton, Sinularia, Dendronephthya*); shrimps, crabs, lobsters and barnacles (Crustacea); clams and other bivalves (Bivalvia); sea slugs (Nudibranchia); sea urchins (Echinoidea); starfish (Astroidea); and sea squirts (Ascidiacea).

MARINE BIOTOPES

DESIGNING THE SIMULATION

This is the most difficult marine biotope to simulate successfully. The majority of invertebrates are extremely sensitive and require optimum water conditions at all times. A great number are also light-loving as they carry algae within their tissues to provide them with a constant supply of the nourishment so lacking in their natural environment.

In trying to simulate a small piece of reef in an aquarium we cannot hope to copy the vast number of food chains and life cycles that make the reef what it is. What we can do is create a reef wall sloping upwards from the bottom front to the top back of the aquarium. Crevices, caves, and overhangs can be duplicated by careful arrangement of the basic rockwork. Sessile invertebrates can be sited appropriately to their normal location on the reef.

Any fish added to the system must be compatible with the invertebrates and their waste should not pollute the water. Consequently, fish stocking levels must be kept low at 2.5cm (1in) of fish per 27 litres (6 gal.) of water.

Water parameters: Ammonia, nitrite, phosphate: 0; pH: 8.2–8.3; Specific gravity: 1.021–1.026; calcium: 400–450ppm; KH: 7; dissolved oxygen: 7–8ppm; redox potential: 350–400mv.
Temperature: 25–26°C (77–80°F).

DÉCOR

Substrate: Substrate material may accumulate detritus, so is probably best completely omitted. Algae and/or sessile invertebrates can be encouraged to grow over the bare glass, or the rockwork can be brought right to the front.
Background: As the wall will obscure much of the back glass, it is best covered with an exterior layer of nontoxic black paint or black plastic.
Main décor: Unlike in freshwater aquaria, it is the actual animals themselves that provide the main decoration. Corals should be positioned so that supporting rockwork remains largely hidden. Given the extent of the rockwork required, tufa rock, being lightweight, is generally used.

Algae will flourish in a tank such as this and may even prove invasive. There are many species of *Caulerpa* which can be introduced once the tank is established.

Caulerpa

Red algae

1–4 are hand-drawn illustrations as opposed to photographs as the use of live coral would be inappropriate.

1. Place invertebrates and rock directly onto the bare glass bottom of the tank.

2. Glue rock foundations together with silicone to prevent slipping or falling.

3. Place the coral so as to obscure the rocks.

4. Plant Caulerpa *and other marine plants for the 'soft furnishing'.*

1

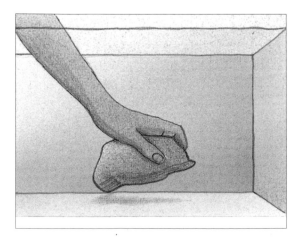

2

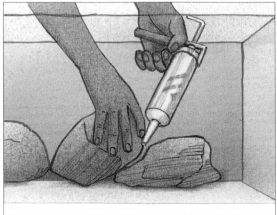

EQUIPMENT

For this type of aquarium it is preferable to use only the most sophisticated equipment available. An aquarium of 120cm (48in) or more in length is desirable, with a minimum volume of 190 litres (42 gal.).

Filtration: Biological filtration should consist of a trickle filter or similar advanced system. Undergravel and other 'simple' filters are not recommended, but proprietary systems are now available as 'complete' units which deserve investigation. There must also be an efficient protein skimmer, preferably connected to ozone, and activated carbon. An ultraviolet sterilizer will help protect the fish from disease, as the use of copper-based medications will prove highly toxic to both invertebrates and any decorative algae. A calcium-dosing system will assist hard corals.

Lighting: Ideally metal halide pendant spot lamps should be employed. A 120cm (48in) tank will require two 150-watt lamps rated at 6,500 or 10,000 Kelvin.

SETTING UP

The rockwork should be structured as for the rocky lake shore (see page 109). However, if no substrate is used special measures are needed to ensure its stability. An all-over (front-to-back and end-to-end) rock foundation should provide the necessary stability, or alternatively the foundation rocks can be stuck to the bottom with silicone sealant.

Most of the visible décor, however, will be living invertebrates, and their individual needs must be carefully researched before siting and positioning.

Protein skimmer

Colourful coral

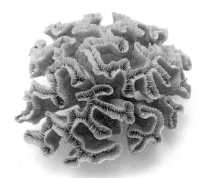

Brain coral – skeleton

Rock

Shell for hermit crab

MAINTENANCE

Regular maintenance is essential and should include regular partial water changes (15 to 25%) every two weeks.

Regular testing will alert the hobbyist to any build-up of nitrates or traces of ammonia or nitrite which could prove fatal to many of the animals. Invertebrates and fish will need to be checked daily for health and the majority will require feeding at the same time.

A complex aquarium of this nature will rely heavily on the equipment it employs, and any malfunction is cause for serious concern as livestock may perish failing speedy rectification of the problem. A good range of spares is essential.

3

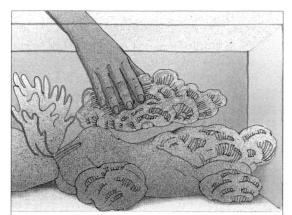

4

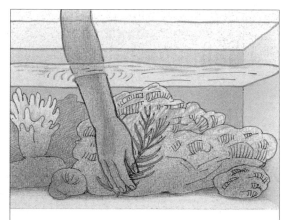

MARINE BIOTOPES

A TRUE CORAL REEF BIOTOPE TANK

BIOTOPE 6 - EELGRASS BEDS

Habitat simulated: All warm seas where coral reefs are abundant have quiet shallow, generally flat-bottomed lagoons protected from the full force of waves and fierce tidal runs by the reef itself. Here we find beds of eel grass and algae growing in abundance. Plants such as these provide excellent cover for certain fish and invertebrates, some of which are superbly camouflaged for protection.

Natural examples: The Great Barrier Reef, coral atolls and islands throughout the tropical seas of the world. Important features: shallow, clear, nutrient-poor water where turbulence is weak and much of the dissolved oxygen is generated by plants: in essence, a 'quiet' location providing an ideal home for less mobile fish. Although large predatory fish visit this portion of the reef, such incursions are generally limited to certain times when the tide is high and they are feeling particularly hungry or inquisitive.

TYPICAL FISH

Seahorses and pipe-fish (Syngnathidae), mandarinfish and dragonets (Callionymidae), and some blennies (Blenniidae).

Pipefish (Syngnathidae)

Crowned seahorse (Hippocampus *sp.*)

A male blenny, Ecsenius australianus

A female blenny, Ecsenius bathi

Yellow banded blenny
(Petroscirites breviceps)

Psychedelic fish
(Synchiropus picturatus)

Dactylopus dactylopus, *a dragonet species*

Mandarinfish
(Synchiropus splendidus)

MARINE BIOTOPES

DESIGNING THE SIMULATION

A biotope such as this lends itself perfectly to the deep sandy bed of an undergravel filter: a flat area of sand where algae can grow unchecked. Eelgrass may not be available in all countries but algae such as *Caulerpa* spp. are reasonably common everywhere and can be used exclusively. It is envisaged that seahorses will be able to find attachment points on the many algal fronds while the pipefish weave in and out and over the plants. Bottom-dwelling fish such as dragonets and mandarinfish may require small algae-free areas. They tend to do very well in the absence of more competitive species.

Water parameters: Ammonia and nitrite: 0;
nitrate: less than 15ppm;
phosphate: less than 0.5ppm;
pH: 8.1–8.3;
specific gravity: 1.021–1.023;
calcium: 250–450ppm;
KH 7 dkH;
dissolved oxygen: 6–8ppm.
Temperature: 25°C (77–78°F).

DÉCOR

Substrate: Coral sand over coral gravel, although the objective is to obscure it as the plants multiply.
Background: The back of the tank will look effective if painted externally in black or a shade of green/blue.
Main décor: Marine plants. Eelgrasses and *Caulerpa* spp. are typical plants of this biotope. If eelgrass is not available, various types of *Caulerpa* will suffice.

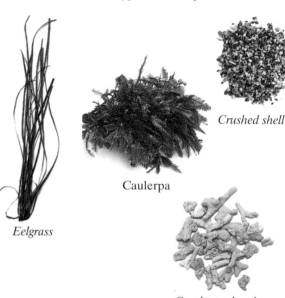

Crushed shell

Caulerpa

Eelgrass

Coral gravel and coral chip mixed

1 Add the first layer of substrate, coral sand or coral gravel.

2 Lay the gravel tidy.

EQUIPMENT

An aquarium which has a large base area is preferable, e.g. 120 x 60cm (48 x 24in). Any depth from 35 to 45cm (14 to 18in) is acceptable.

Filtration: A standard UG system covering the entire bottom will provide adequate biological filtration. Several uplifts can be positioned along the back of the tank, or one in each corner if preferred. These may be powered by air, or preferably powerheads.

Supporting filtration must include a protein skimmer and activated carbon in a canister filter. Ozone is not strictly necessary as any residual amounts contaminating the tank water will prove harmful to the algae. An ultraviolet sterilizer will be required to help control any disease organisms as copper medication will also prove toxic to plant growth.

Lighting: Lighting need not be intense and three fluorescent tubes will be sufficient. Alternatively, two 80-watt mercury vapour spot lamps will lend a more realistic feeling to the underwater scene.

SETTING UP

The undergravel filter plates should cover the entire base of the aquarium. On top of these place coral gravel at a rate of approximately 4kg (8.5 lb) per 900cm^2 (1ft^2).

A gravel tidy must then be installed between this and the next layer of substrate: coral sand at the rate of about 8kg (17 lb) per 900cm^2 (1ft^2), to give the required depth of 10cm (4in). It is recommended that a second gravel tidy be installed to prevent digging fish short-circuiting the main filter bed, and this should be fitted after half the thickness of coral sand has been added.

MAINTENANCE

Apart from the obligatory water changes, successfully maintaining a tank of this nature requires that the fish are fed correctly.

Seahorses and pipefish are notoriously finicky and prefer live foods wherever possible, so a continuous supply of live brine shrimp (*Artemia*) must be cultured. Dragonets and mandarinfish will benefit from the same foods.

3 Add sea water after two layers of substrate.

4 Plant the eelgrass and Caulerpa.

MARINE BIOTOPES

AN EELGRASS BED BIOTOPE TANK

BIOTOPE 7 - THE SANDY PLAIN

Habitat simulated: A common feature found within the confines of many coral reefs is the flat sandy plain. At first glance it may appear to be lifeless but many creatures have adapted to live in this featureless environment. Many people are unaware that coral sand is not always the work of wave erosion. In fact, much of it is produced by fish! Parrotfish, in particular, use their strong jaws to continuously scrape away at the calcareous rocks and corals in a bid to extract sustenance from the algae contained therein. The waste material is expelled from their gills as coral sand and gathers in gullies which channel it onto the flat plains and lagoons.

Natural examples: All the locations mentioned for Biotope Five possess adjacent sandy plains.

Important features: The sandy plain is largely flat, sometimes undulating, with a few rocks scattered here and there. The soft sand is deep and can be used by burrowing animals to construct extensive retreats. Some areas may also develop large 'pastures' of eelgrass or algae as we have already seen, forming an effectively separate biotope.

TYPICAL FISH

Jawfish (Opistognathidae), Goatfish (Mullidae), some blennies (Blenniidae), bottom-dwelling rays (class Chondrichthys, many families), seahorses (Syngnathidae), some gobies (Gobiidae), dragonets (Callionymidae) and rabbitfish (Siganidae).

Most of these fish either burrow in the sand for protection or sift it for food particles, or both.

Garden eels (Heterocongridae) are reasonably common in sandy lagoons. They live in large colonies and occupy a vertical burrow about an eel's length from their neighbour. At the first sign of danger, they retreat into their burrows tail-first. Note that these eels are not suitable aquarium inhabitants, and are mentioned here only as typical inhabitants of the sandy plain.

Molluscs, starfish, sea cucumbers and sea urchins, as well as a myriad worms and crustaceans, live above and below the sand.

Such a bountiful supply of food does not go unnoticed by predators such as rays and triggerfish, and they spend much of their time hunting over this part of the reef complex. Other fish may be tempted to search for food here – however they would soon be noticed by predators and eaten themselves!

Banded blenny (Salaria fasciatus)

Blacksaddle goatfish (Parupeneus rubescens)

Garden eels (Gorgasia maculata) *protruding from seabed burrows*

Rabbitfishes (Siganus *sp.*)

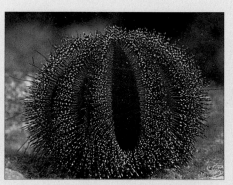

Sea urchin (Mespilia globulus)

Goatfish (Parupeneus forsskali)

DESIGNING THE SIMULATION

Obviously the emphasis here will be on creating a large, flat sandy area. Perhaps one or two large rocks could be placed here and there to add interest and an area of marine algae or eelgrass would supply some extra cover and colour.

Water parameters: Unlike the coral reef tank, we are not considering invertebrates here and consequently there can be some flexibility in water parameters as described under that heading. Whilst ammonia and nitrite must always remain at zero, nitrate is permissible to a maximum of 25ppm, as are phosphates which should not exceed 0.5ppm. Calcium levels may fall as low as 250ppm.

The remaining parameters must remain the same.

DÉCOR

Substrate: Coral sand over coral gravel – although the objective is largely to obscure it as the plants multiply.

Background: As the rear panel of the aquarium will be fully visible, a background is both necessary and desirable. There are several options: paint it (externally) a suitable colour; stick black plastic sheeting over it; or stick on a proprietary plastic photobackground. The choice is a subjective one and best left to the personal taste of the individual hobbyist.

Coral sand

Eelgrass

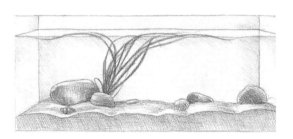

1 Sculpt a shape to the substrate to resemble the corrugations formed by the tides. The surface may not stay exactly like this after the fish have been introduced but the basic form should remain.

2 Scattered stones add interest and are objects for crabs to climb over.

EQUIPMENT

The best aquarium to use will be a rather shallow one, perhaps 35 to 45cm (14 to 18in) deep, but having a reasonable base area, say 180 x 60cm (72 x 24in).

Filtration: Biological filtration by undergravel filters, as for Biotope Six (see page 135). A protein skimmer remains an essential piece of equipment, as does a facility for housing activated carbon.

An ultraviolet sterilizer should be installed to help protect the fish from harmful diseases.

Lighting: Two or three full-length fluorescent tubes will provide more than adequate illumination. Two 125-watt mercury vapour spot lamps will present the scene in a more realistic fashion as the ripples of light play over the surface of the sand.

SETTING UP

The undergravel filter plates should cover the entire base of the aquarium. On top of these place coral gravel at a rate of approximately 4kg (8.5 lb) per 900cm^2 (1ft^2).

A gravel tidy must then be installed between this and the next layer of substrate: coral sand at the rate of about 8kg (17 lb) per ft^2, to give the required depth of 10cm (4in).

It is recommended that a second gravel tidy be installed to prevent digging fish short-circuiting the main filter bed, and this should be fitted after half the thickness of coral sand has been added.

Rocks

MAINTENANCE

Apart from the usual 15 to 25% water changes every two weeks, very little maintenance is necessary. The sand may need to be occasionally raked flat as the fish disturb it. However, every effort must be made to avoid destroying any burrows that fish are currently occupying.

3 Fill the tank halfway and then plant the eelgrass.

4 Release the fish into matured tank water.

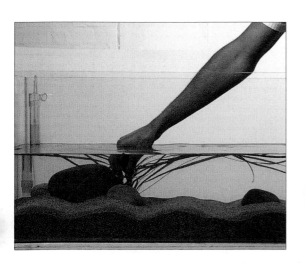

MARINE BIOTOPES

A SANDY PLAIN BIOTOPE TANK

BIOTOPE 8 - OPEN WATER NEAR THE REEF

Habitat simulated: If we discount the coral wall and the sandy lagoon, the open water around the reef nevertheless remains a place of interest. Fish abound in this open space, feeding on plankton, invertebrates and even other fish.

Natural examples: All coral reefs have open areas of water where fish congregate.

Important features: Apart from providing as much swimming space as possible, the only other requirement is a place for each species to shelter. Very few non-nocturnal fish remain in open water at night – they generally retreat to the safety of the coral wall or dive into the sand.

TYPICAL FISH

Surgeonfish (Acanthuridae), triggerfish (Balistidae), butterflyfish (Chaetodontidae), porcupinefish (Diodontidae), batfish (Ephippidae), wrasse (Labridae), boxfish (Ostraciidae), sweetlips (Haemulidae), angelfish (Pomacanthidae), lionfish (Scorpaenidae), rabbitfish (Siganidae) and pufferfish (Tetraodontidae).

Cowfish (Lactoria cornuta)

Rectangular triggerfish (Rhinecanthus rectangulus)

Chevroned butterflyfish (Chaetodon trifascialis)

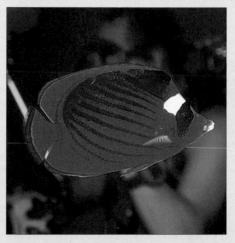

Raccoon butterflyfish (Chaetodon fasciatus)

Majestic angelfish (Pomacanthus navarchus)

Sweetlips (Plectorhinchus gaterinus)

Powder-blue surgeonfish (Acanthurus leucosternon)

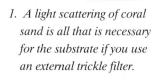

DESIGNING THE SIMULATION

When we try to recreate this biotope in the confines of the aquarium, we find that a certain amount of adaptation is called for. Most aquarists do not want just a glass box full of water with a few fish swimming around. Most would like to at least try to represent the reef wall by building up rockwork, albeit without corals, to cover a large area of the back of the aquarium, while leaving as much swimming space to the front as possible.

An important point to bear in mind is that only a finite number of fish can be kept in any aquarium. A sandy plain (Biotope Seven) or fish-only aquarium has a maximum stocking density of 2.5cm (1in) of fish for every 9 litres (2 gal.) of water. This must be gradually built up over a period of a year.

Water parameters: As for the Sandy Plain biotope (see page 140).

1. A light scattering of coral sand is all that is necessary for the substrate if you use an external trickle filter.

2. Place the rocks against the back wall to allow space for swimming in the front of the tank.

DÉCOR

Substrate: If external trickle filtration is utilized then a light scattering of coral sand will be all that is necessary. However, an area of deeper sand can be provided, partitioned off (using glass strips siliconed to the tank base to create an enclosure about 2.5–5cm; 1–2in deep) to provide a nighttime retreat for wrasses, if required. On the other hand, an undergravel filter will provide the necessary deep sandy substrate.

Background: The rocky wall at the rear of the aquarium will provide all the background necessary.

Main décor: Apart from the main rockwork, artificial corals can be positioned to provide further interest, as can dried sea fans and sea whips. Empty shells are also very decorative. It must be stressed here that algae will undoubtedly cover any decorative items introduced and change their appearance, which, although quite natural, may prove unacceptable.

Shells add colour

Tufa rock

1

2

EQUIPMENT

The minimum tank length recommended for this biotope is 120cm (48in).

Filtration: The sophistication of the filtration system will depend largely upon which fish are to be kept. Large, hungry fish will require an efficient system capable of ridding the water of equally

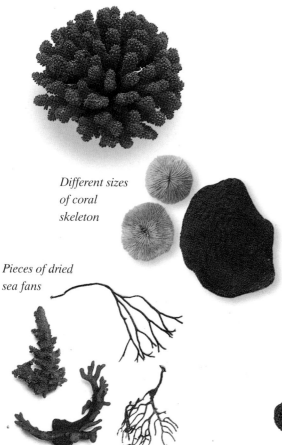

Different sizes of coral skeleton

Pieces of dried sea fans

3

large quantities of waste very quickly. This may involve an undertank trickle filter, a large protein skimmer, and a separate filter to reduce nitrate (a denitrator).

A collection of smaller fish can flourish with an undergravel filter and an efficient protein skimmer. In both cases, activated carbon must be included in the system.

An ultraviolet sterilizer of a suitable wattage must be installed to reduce disease pathogens that might otherwise multiply out of control and threaten the health of the fish.

Lighting: In the case of this biotope, lighting is required only to permit proper viewing of the fish and to present the display attractively, and is largely a matter of individual taste. Fluorescent tubes, mercury vapour and metal halide lamps are all acceptable.

SETTING UP

The process of setting up has largely been described under the two preceding headings, depending on whether undergravel or trickle filters are employed. The rockwork can be erected as for Biotope Two (see page 108).

Shells

4

3. *Arrange the other décor items around the rocks.*

4. *Add water by siphoning sea water from a bucket and pouring it onto a plate so as not to disturb the substrate.*

MARINE BIOTOPES

OPEN WATER NEAR THE REEF BIOTOPE TANK

CONSERVATION NOTE

Of all the natural biotopes we have looked at, the coral reef is perhaps the most complex and difficult to emulate in captivity. Every reef is highly sensitive to even the smallest changes in temperature, pH and salinity. Pollutants such as nitrates and phosphates are almost nonexistent in the wild and their introduction can have a devastating affect on all the animals and plants which inhabit these wonderful areas of the world.

With the advent of global warming and the increase in tourism to these delicate ecosystems, some coral reefs are coming under a great deal of pressure; animals are dying for reasons that are not readily apparent, algae is smothering the corals and the water can be so cloudy that it blocks out the light from the sun. When designing our coral reef biotope, we would do well to remember that keeping fish from these ecologically sensitive areas places a great responsibility on the marine fishkeeper. No longer is it acceptable to lose fish or invertebrates while experimenting with different systems or through failing to perform vital maintenance tasks.

Captive-bred species account for only a minute percentage of the marine animals available through the aquarium trade. The vast majority are still collected directly from the reef, and we must therefore make every effort to preserve every fish or invertebrate we buy; if we lose one, the chances are high that it will have to be replaced directly from the reef!

However, that is not to say we should be discouraged from taking up the marine hobby or enjoying it to the full. We would merely suggest that the novice fishkeeper plan his or her aquarium carefully and well in advance. Marine fish and invertebrates are very unforgiving of the mistakes commonly made by aquarists trying to make too much progress, too quickly and too soon.

Further, while it is not strictly necessary – provided strict attention is paid to every fine detail – there is a lot to be said for learning the basics of fishkeeping, especially as regards water chemistry and quality, via a freshwater aquarium in the first instance.

CONCLUSION

Our book, like the river, has reached its end; but not, we hope, the end of its usefulness and interest. We hope that we have demonstrated that an aquarium can – and should – be far more than just a glass box containing a few fish and plants. Even the general community will benefit from attention to natural detail, and the creation of biotope aquaria will ensure continuing interest for years to come.

As you begin your fishkeeping career you will undoubtedly be confused by all there is to learn, but in a few years' time you will find you have become a chemist and zoologist and perhaps a botanist, a geologist, and all sorts of other 'ologists', as well as an electrician, carpenter, plumber and so on. We hope our book will help you on your way, and still be a source of interest and ideas when you are in turn an expert aquarist.

Right *Butterfly cichlids* (Papiliochromis ramirezi).

APPENDIX

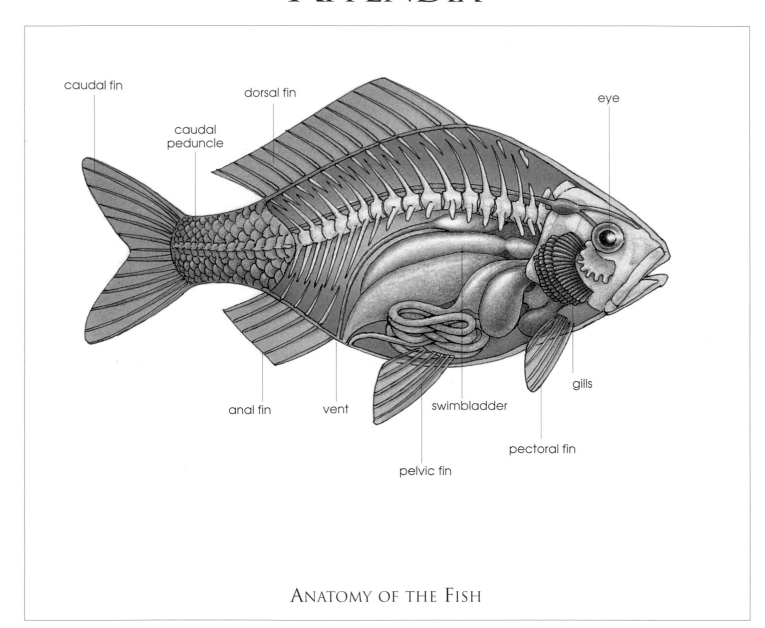

caudal fin

dorsal fin

eye

caudal
peduncle

anal fin

vent

swimbladder

gills

pectoral fin

pelvic fin

ANATOMY OF THE FISH

Apistogramma borellii 101
Apogonidae *91, 129*
Apolemichthys
  trimaculatus 95
Apteronotidae *80*
Archamia fucata 127
Arius jordani 83
Arothron diadematus 90
Astatotilapia burtoni 73
Astronotus 101

Balistapus undulatus 89
Balistidae *89, 129, 139, 145*
Balistoides conspicillum 37
Balitoridae *82*
Barbus bimaculatus 82
Barbus tetrazona 66
Belontia hasselti 86
Belontidae *86*
Betta splendens 77
Blenniidae *88, 129, 133, 139*
Brachydanio rerio 82

Callionymidae *133, 134, 139*
Campylomormyrus
  rhynchophorus 80
Chaetodon auriga 145
Chaetodon fasciatus 145
Chaetodon semilarvatus 88
Chaetodon unimaculatus
  interruptus 34
Chaetodon unimaculatus
  unimaculatus 34
Chaetodontidae *88, 129,*
  145
Channa argus 80
Characidae *36, 78, 81, 101*
Cichlidae *69, 78, 85, 86,*
  101, 103, 107, 113, 119
Cirrhitidae *90, 129*
Cirrhitus splendens 90
Cleithracara 101
Cobitidae *82*
Crenicichla sp. 35
Cyphotilapia frontosa 85
Cyprinidae *82*

Cyprinodontidae *84*
Cyrtocara moorii 78

Dactylopus dactylopus 133
Dimidiochromis
  compressiceps 85
Diodon liturosus 90
Diodontidae *90, 145*
Dysichthys 101

Ecsenius australianus 133
Ecsenius bathi 88, 133
Eigenmannia virescens 80
Electrophorus electricus 97
Ephippidae *145*
Epinephelus sp. 96
Epiplatys fasciolatus 35
Etroplus maculatus 86

Forcipiger flavissimus 127

Gasteropelecidae *79, 81,*
  101
Gasteropelecus sternicla
  36
Geophagus brasiliensis 85
Gobiidae *91, 119*
Gobiodon citrinus 91
Gorgasia maculata 139
Gramma loreto 92
Grammidae *92, 129*
Gyrinocheilus aymonieri
  82

Haemulidae *145*
Haplochromis burtoni 73
Hemichromis guttatus 60, 71
Heteroconger hassi 139
Heterocongridae *139*
Hippocampus sp. 133
Holocentridae *127*
Hyphessobrycon callistus
  callistus 81
Hyphessobrycon griemi 81

Julidochromis regani 107

Labeo 82, 113
Labidochromis caeruleus 107
Labridae *92, 129, 145*
Labroides dimidiatus 66
Lactoria cornuta 145
Laetacara 101
Lebiasinidae *79, 81, 101*

Macropodus opercularis 86
Malapterurus electricus 97
Mastacembelus
  erythrotaenia 80, 113
Megalodoras irwini 35
Melanochromis auratus 107
Melanochromis chipokae 32
Melanotaenia boesemani 80
Melanotaenia splendida 119
Melanotaenia trifasciata
  80, 119
Melanotaenidae *80*
Microdesmidae *93, 127*
Monodactylidae *86*
Monodactylus argenteus
  119
Mormyridae *80, 113*
Mullidae *139*
Muraenidae *93, 127*

Nandidae *80*
Nanochromis nudiceps
  113
Nemateleotris magnifica 93
Neolamprologus
  tretocephalus 107
Nothobranchius patrizii 84
Nothobranchius rachovii 84
Nothobranchius sp. 101
Notopteridae *80*

Opistognathidae *94, 139*
Opistognathus aurifrons 94
Orthochromis machadoi
  68, 113
Osphronemus goramy 86
Osteochilus vittatus 82
Osteoglossidae *80*

Ostraciidae *94, 145*
Ostracion cubicus 94
Ostracion sp. 94
Oxycirrhites typus 90

Panaque nigrolineatus 83
Pangasius sutchii 66
Pantodon buchholtzi 80
Pantodontidae *80*
Paracanthurus hepatus 87
Paracheirodon innesi 101
Parupeneus forsskali 139
Parupeneus rubescens 139
Pelvicachromis taeniatus
  85, 101
Petroscirites breviceps 88,
  133
Phenacogrammus
  interruptus 81
Piaractus brachypomus 81
Plectorhynchus
  chaetodontoides 66
Plectorhynchus gaterinus
  145
Plesiopidae *96, 129*
Poecilia nigrofasciata 84
Poeciliidae *84*
Polyodon spathula 35
Pomacanthidae *95, 101,*
  129, 145, 147
Pomacanthus imperator 95
Pomacanthus navarchus 145
Pomacentridae *30, 95, 129*
Pseudocheilinus
  hexataenia 92
Pseudochromidae *92*
Pseudochromis porphyreus
  92
Pseudotropheus estherae
  107
Pseudotropheus lombardoi
  107
Pterois volitans 96, 132, 145
Pterophyllum scalare 37,
  77, 101
Pygoplites diacanthus 95

Rasbora heteromorpha
  82, 101
Rhinecanthus rectangulus
  145
Rivulus sp. 101

Scatophagidae *86, 119*
Scorpaenidae *96, 132, 145*
Semaprochilodus taeniurus
  81
Serranidae *96*
Serrasalmus nattereri 81
Siganidae *139, 145*
Siganus sp. 139
Siluriformes *83, 97, 101,*
  113, 119
Sphaeramia nematopterus
  91
Steatocranus irvinei 113
Steatocranus ubanguiensis
  113
Symphysodon
  aequifasciatus 68, 85, 101
Symphysodon 101
Synchiropus splendidus 89,
  133
Synchiropus picturatus 89,
  133
Syngnathidae *97, 133, 134,*
  139
Synodontis angelicus 83
Synodontis multipunctatus
  107

Teleogramma brichardi 113
Tetraodontidae *86, 90,*
119, 145
Thayeria boehlkei 81
Toxotidae *86, 119, 120,*
123
Triglachromis otostigma 35

Uaru 35, 101
Uaru amphicanthoides 35

Valenciennea strigata 91

GLOSSARY

absorption: the process of taking in and retaining; much like a sponge takes in water.

activated carbon: carbon that has been fired a second time at very high temperatures to increase its porosity and thus provide an even greater surface area.

adsorption: the process by which a solid takes up other substances on to its surface.

airstone: a type of diffuser made of a material resembling stone in texture.

allopatric: having a different geographical range.

ballast unit: the control gear for fluorescent, mercury vapour or metal halide lighting.

biotope: a habitat together with its flora and fauna.

brackish water: water which is neither totally fresh (salt-free) nor fully salt (i.e. sea water); usually used to describe the dilute salt water found where the sea and fresh water mingle.

cable tidy: a small electrical control unit into which a number of devices can be wired so as to connect them to a single mains outlet.

conspecific: belonging to the same species.

cornering (of fish bags): to round off the corners (with tape, rubber bands) to prevent fish from becoming trapped/injured in them.

diffuser: a small piece of equipment used to split the current of air from an air pump into a large number of small bubbles, for aeration purposes. Usually made of limewood, plastic, or a stone-like composite.

double bagging: packing fish in doubled plastic bags (one inside another) to guard against leaks.

emerse: out of water.

epiphytic: growing on plants.

fluviatile: of rivers.

gang valves: a set of two or more linked control valves used to split an aquarium air supply between multiple outlets.

gorgonians: an encompassing term to describe sea whips and sea fans.

gravel tidy: a (usually plastic) mesh used to separate layers of different types of substrate material, or to prevent fish from digging down to the bottom of the aquarium.

heterospecific: belong to a different species.

hydrometer: an instrument used to measure salinity.

inert: chemically inactive.

interspecific: between different species.

intraspecific: within a species.

KH: carbonate hardness.

lacustrine: of lakes.

marginal (of plants): growing along the edge of a body of water, usually with at least the roots, and sometimes part of the stem/leaves in water, without the whole plant being fully submerged.

metabolism: the combined life processes of a living organism.

nitrogen cycle: the natural cycle relating to the transformation of nitrogen and nitrogenous (containing nitrogen) compounds in relation to living organisms. In aquarium terminology usually restricted to the breakdown (nitrification) of organic wastes.

ozone (O_3): a gas, an unstable, allotropic, form of oxygen: the ozone molecule consists of three oxygen atoms instead of the normal two of gaseous oxygen (O_2).

pathogen: an organism that causes disease.

pH: a universally recognized measurement of acidity and alkalinity.

powerhead: a submersible pump specially designed for powering some types of aquarium filters, especially undergravel.

pump impeller: the rotary unit that forces water through a pump.

redox potential: a measurement of water's ability to cleanse itself. Recorded in millivolts.

reverse osmosis: a process used to purify water of both organic and inorganic contaminants, producing almost pure H_2O.

rheophilic: current loving.

RO: abbreviation for Reverse Osmosis.

salinity: the measure of the sodium chloride (NaCl) content of a liquid (usually water).

spawning mop: an artificial (usually home-made) spawning medium, generally consisting of a bunch of wool or nylon strands attached to a cork (floating mop) or pebble (non-floating mop).

specific gravity (SG): in an aquarium context, a measure of the salinity of water.

strengthening bars: strips of material, usually glass, sometimes plastic, used to add rigidity to the top rim of an all-glass aquarium. They may run along the individual panes to strengthen them, or centrally across the long axis of the aquarium to prevent outward bowing.

spawning substrate: any item (plant, rock, aquarium glass, etc.) on which fish eggs are laid.

substrate: the term used to describe the material found on the bottom of both a biotope and an aquarium.

surfactants: organic and inorganic substances which are readily dissolved in salt water, but are easily drawn to the interface between air and water.

swim bladder: a special gas-filled organ in fishes, which provides them with buoyancy.

sympatric: having a shared or overlapping geographical distribution.

syntopic: sharing the same biotope.

taxonomy: the science of the classification of living things.

Terry clips: roughly circular metal spring clips, open at one end, attached to a surface at the other, used to hold roughly circular objects in place, eg. fluorescent tubes, tools, hoses and cables (eg. in the car engine compartment).

T-piece: T-shaped pieces of rigid plastic tube used to split an air supply into two, without any flow control. See 'gang valves'.

UG: abbreviation for Under Gravel filter.

uplift: the vertical pipe used in some types of internal filters, through which water is drawn upwards prior to being returned to the aquarium.

water chemistry: the chemical composition of (the contaminants in) any given sample of water, i.e. the substances, organic and inorganic, dissolved in it. In aquarium terminology usually restricted to inorganic substances.

water quality: the measure of the presence or absence of undesirable and potentially harmful materials (in the aquarium sense, chiefly organic) in a sample of water.

water parameters: the required, or existing, levels of certain elements of water chemistry and quality (usually pH, hardness, and nitrogenous compounds, but sometimes also including specific inorganics, eg. sodium chloride, copper).

BIBLIOGRAPHY

Breder, C.M. & Rosen, D.E. 1966 *Modes of Reproduction in Fishes*, TFH Publications, Neptune City, NJ, USA

Burgess, P.J., Bailey, M.C., and Exell, A. 1998 *A-Z of tropical fish diseases and problems* (due out November 1998), Ringpress Books, Lydney, UK

Burgess, W.E. 1989 *An Atlas of Freshwater and Marine Catfishes*, TFH Publications, Neptune City, NJ, USA

Burgess, W.E. 1988 *An Atlas of Marine Aquarium Fishes*, TFH Publications, Neptune City, NJ, USA

Cannon, L. & Goyen, M. 1990 *Australia's Great Barrier Reef*, Watermark Press, Australia

Dakin, N. 1992 *The Book of the Marine Aquarium*, Salamander Books, London, UK

Dakin, N. 1996 *The Question & Answers Manual of The Marine Aquarium*, Andromeda Books, Oxford, UK

Debelius, H. 1993 *Indian Ocean Tropical Fish Guide*, Aquaprint, Germany

Fossa, S. and Nilsen, A.J. 1996 *The Modern Coral Reef Aquarium*, Vol. I and II, BSV, Germany

Fryer, G. and Iles, T.D. 1972 *The Cichlid Fishes of the Great Lakes of Africa*, Oliver & Boyd, London & Edinburgh

Géry, J. 1977 *Characoids of the World*, TFH Publications, Neptune City, NJ, USA

Golding, M. 1989 *Amazon, The Flooded Forest*, BBC Books, UK

Greenwood, P.H. 1975 *A History of Fishes*, Ernest Benn Ltd, London, UK

Konings, A. 1995 *Malawi Cichlids in their Natural Habitat*, 2nd Edition, Cichlid Press: www.cichlidpress.com

Konings, A. 1998 *Tanganyika Cichlids in their Natural Habitat*, Cichlid Press: www.cichlidpress.com

Linke, H. and Staeck, W. 1995 *African Cichlids I: Cichlids from West Africa*, Tetra Press, Germany

Linke, H. and Staeck, W. 1995 *American Cichlids I: Dwarf Cichlids*, Tetra Press, Germany

Lowe-McConnell, R.H. 1987 *Ecological Studies in Tropical Fish Communities*, Cambridge University Press, UK

Merrick, J.R. and Schmeider, G.E. 1987 *Australian Freshwater Fishes*, Macquarie University, Australia

Mühlberg, H. 1980 *The Complete Guide to Water Plants*, EPP Publishing Ltd

Reed, G.M. 1989 *The Living Waters of Korup Rainforest*, WWF report 3206/A8:1

Riehl, R. and Baensch, H.A. 1987 *Aquarium Atlas* Vol.I, Vol.II (1993), Vol.III (1994), Mergus Verlag, Germany

Scheel, J.J. 1990 *Atlas of the Killifishes of the Old World*, TFH Publications, Neptune City, New York

Seuss, W. 1993 *Corydoras*, Dähne Verlag, Germany

Sioli, H. (Ed.) 1984 *The Amazon: Limnology and Landscape Ecology of a Mighty Tropical River and its Basin*, Dr W. Junk Publishers, Dordrecht & Boston

Stawikowski, R. and Werner, U. 1998 *Die Buntbarsche Amerikas*, Vol.I, Eugen Ulmer, Germany

Sterba, G. 1967 *Freshwater Fishes of the World*, Studio Vista, London

Thresher, Dr R.E. 1984 *Reproduction In Reef Fishes*, TFH Publications, Neptune City, NJ, USA

Wickler, W. 1966 *Breeding Aquarium Fishes*, Studio Vista, London

Zupanc, G.K.H. 1985 *Fish and their Behaviour*, Tetra, Germany

In addition, two German Publishers are progressively publishing pictorial guides to families of freshwater fishes. The AQUALOG (ACS Glaser) and AQUALEX (Dähne) series are bilingual, English/German. At the time of writing guides are available on groups of cichlids, catfishes, as well as characins, livebearers and killifishes.

PHOTOGRAPHIC CREDITS

All photographs by Anthony Johnson for the Struik Image Library (SIL) except for those supplied by photographers or agencies as listed below:

ABPL: pp. 87 bottom; 93 bottom right (Peter Pinnock).

Bailey, Mary: pp. 8 bottom; 32 centre and bottom right; 35 top right; below right; below left and bottom left; 43 bottom right; 47 top left; 3rd below left; bottom left and centre right; 48 bottom; 59 bottom; 68 top and bottom; 72 top; 75; 78 bottom; 84 bottom left; 85 top middle and right, bottom; 101 top left, top right and bottom right; 107 top, centre, below left-to-right; 113 top, centre top, centre bottom, bottom left and right.

BIOS: p. 3; (Remy Gantes); pp. 38/39; 41 top; 85 centre (Yvette Tavernier).

Branch, G.M.: pp. 34 top and bottom; 119 bottom left.

Bruce Coleman Ltd.: pp. 66 top left; 71; 73; 133 bottom right (Jane Burton); p. 81 top left (Hector Rivarola).

Dakin, Nick: pp. 20; 21; 22; 24; 42 right; 43 centre; 47 bottom right; 65 centre; 70; 87 top left; 89 bottom left and right; 91 top and bottom left; 92 top left; top right and bottom left; 94 top left; 127 top right, centre right; bottom middle, bottom right.

Griffiths, Charles: pp. 33 bottom; 91 bottom right; 92 bottom right; 119 top; 145 top left.

Hes, Lex: p. 118.

Huchzermeyer, Dr K D A: pp. 67; 68 centre; 69 top, centre and bottom.

King, D.: back cover flap (top); pp. 18/19 centre; 32 top; 33 top; 87 top right and centre; 88 bottom left; 90 bottom centre; 95 top left; 97 top right; 127 top left; 133 top right; 144.

Köhler, Danja: pp. 37 top left; 66 bottom; 88 top right and top left; 95 bottom left; 96 bottom; 127 bottom left; 133 centre, left-to-right; 139 top left; 145 centre right and bottom right.

Kuiter, Rudie H.: p. 83 middle.

Mary Evans Picture Library: pp. 8 top; 9 bottom.

NHPA: pp. 4/5 (Gerard Lacz); p. 119 bottom right (Stephen Dalton); p. 132 (Ashod Francis Papazian); pp. 133 bottom middle; 139 centre (B. Jones and M. Shimlock); p. 139 bottom left and 151 (Bill Wood).

Photo Access: front cover, top centre (Planet Earth/Ken Lucas); pp. 12/13 (Gary Bell); p. 17 (Planet Earth/Andre Bartschi); pp. 36 bottom left (Planet Earth/Peter Scoones); 78 left (Mark Conlin); p.90 top left (Pete Atkinson); p. 138 (Planet Earth/Marty Snyderman); p. 139 bottom middle (Pete Atkinson).

Pinnock, Peter: pp. 90 top right; 93 top right and bottom left; 95 centre left; 96 top; 126; 139 top right and bottom right; 145 top right and bottom left.

Sandford, Mike: back cover flap (bottom); pp. 35 bottom right and top right; 72 bottom; 74; 76; 77 top left and top right; 80 top left, top right, centre left, centre right; bottom left and bottom right; 81 top right and bottom right; 82 top, centre, bottom left and bottom right; 83 top and bottom; 84 top, bottom middle and bottom right; 85 top left; 86 top left, top right, bottom left and bottom right; 97 centre and bottom right; 119 centre left and bottom middle; 133 bottom left.

Spiby, Geoff: pp. 30 bottom left; 88 centre right; 89 top; 90 bottom left; 94 bottom left and right; 95 top right and centre right; 95 bottom right; 127 centre left and centre middle; 133 top left; 145 centre left and middle.

Struik Image Library (SIL): p. 112; p. 100 (Andrew Bannister); pp. 98-99 (Gerhard Dreyer); pp. 16; pp. 18 top; 106 (Peter Ribton).